Cultivating Kindness

 in School

**Activities That Promote
Integrity, Respect, and
Compassion in Elementary
and Middle School
Students**

Ric Stuecker

Research Press 2612 North Mattis Avenue • Champaign, Illinois 61822
[800] 519-2707 • www.researchpress.com

Copies of this book may be ordered from Research Press at the address
given on the title page.

Composition by Jeff Helgesen
Cover design by Linda Brown, Positive I.D. Graphic Design, Inc.
Printed by McNaughton & Gunn, Inc.

ISBN 0-87822-485-8
Library of Congress Control Number 2003110820

To Nancy Hugo, whose life-affirming energy inspires all she touches

Contents

Kind Classrooms: Lessons for Grades 4–8 115

Tables

Acknowledgments

The *Cultivating Kindness in School* initiative was inspired by the "It's Kool to be Kind" program at Yorba Linda Middle School in Orange County, California. The idea for that program was suggested by the school Parent Teacher Organization and developed and implemented by the assistant principal, Arthur Cummins. Thanks to everyone involved in that program.

Based on the program at Yorba Linda, the Kindness Initiative described in this book was originally developed for use in the Hugo, Oklahoma, public schools as part of the Safe Schools/Healthy Students Initiative, sponsored by the U.S. Departments of Justice, Education, and Health and Human Services. I extend my gratitude for the sponsorship of these schools and governmental agencies.

I also wish to thank Arthur Cummins and Suze Rutherford for their review and constructive criticism of the manual, as well as for their contributions.

Introduction

The Kindness Initiative described in this book is designed to help youths in elementary and middle schools acquire developmental assets and become more resilient. Its specific purpose is to encourage kind treatment, promote a positive school environment, lower the tension among groups, decrease the number of disciplinary reports, and teach students the social skills they need to be successful adults.

The program approaches these goals in two ways, reflected in this book's two parts: through a schoolwide campaign and through classroom participation in specific learning activities. Part 1 of this book, "Kind Schools," presents plans for schoolwide activities. Part 2, "Kind Classrooms," includes lessons for grades K–3 and grades 4–8. Each of these approaches augments the other in fostering the development of integrity, responsibility, and compassion. Together, these activities and lessons are designed to promote kindness as a way of life. The book also includes three appendixes: Appendix A describes how the Kindness Initiative fits within the context of character education, Appendix B suggests steps toward integrating high school students into the program, and Appendix C gives full-page versions (posters) of items to be displayed during lessons.

FOUNDATION OF THE KINDNESS INITIATIVE

At this point, it is important to know about two aspects of the Kindness Initiative that underlie both the schoolwide and classroom components: the Three Basic Rules and the Kindness Pledge.

Three Basic Rules

In the Kindness Initiative, all students and staff agree to live by three simple rules. As much as possible, staff follow these rules to ensure consistency across classrooms and within the school.

Rule 1: Be Kind to Yourself

When people are kind to themselves, they live lives of personal integrity, responsibility, and compassion. They make sure to know the rules, make positive contributions to their learning community, seek heroes, and reach for the challenges that ultimately will lead to personal success.

Rule 2: Be Kind to One Another

When people are kind to one another, they praise one another's contributions, listen to one another, put down put-downs, heal hurts, honor diversity, resolve conflicts with others, and ask for forgiveness when needed.

Rule 3: Be Kind to This Space

When people are kind to the learning environment, they keep it clean, return materials to their proper places, help put away materials at the end of activities, honor each person's personal property, use materials safely, and pitch in to keep the learning space attractive and clean.

The Kindness Pledge

The Kindness Initiative and the concept of kindness in the school are introduced during the opening weeks of school through the Kindness Pledge, shown in Table 1. Posters of the pledge as a whole and of its individual tenets are displayed prominently throughout the school, and teachers and staff encourage students to live by them. If desired, classes may recite the Kindness Pledge each day after they have recited the pledge of allegiance to the flag.

PART 1: KIND SCHOOLS

By employing schoolwide practices to create a positive school environment, educators enhance the growth occurring in individual classrooms. When children enter the doors of the school, they know that they are entering a special environment that is safe and loving, and that they will be treated fairly and kindly by all the adults they meet. When every person in the school agrees to live by the values of the Kindness Pledge and then does so, the campus climate becomes more positive, adults are less confrontational with students, and students are less aggressive. The school itself becomes a community in which individuals are honored and affirmed. As a result, students are more motivated to strive toward academic success.

Part 1 of this book includes directions in the form of 20 activities that educators may follow to develop a schoolwide campaign that is responsive to the needs of their particular school. The content of these activities ranges from creating a program

TABLE 1

The Kindness Pledge

We are kind to one another by . . .

1. Seeking to be positive
2. Putting down put-downs
3. Honoring our differences
4. Discovering our similarities
5. Healing our hurts
6. Listening to one another
7. Honoring heroes
8. Reaching higher for success
9. Living our dreams

task force and small-group action teams to making posters and creating a group of student speakers to publicize the initiative.

Communities can connect with the school's efforts by promoting the program through the media, actively sponsoring specific projects, and providing guest speakers to address the school and individual classrooms. Schools can encourage learning by engaging parents in the work of the Kindness Initiative and by encouraging them to adopt the tenets of the Kindness Pledge at home.

PART 2: KIND CLASSROOMS

Through the lessons in Part 2, classrooms become learning communities, teachers implement the Three Basic Rules, and students learn the Kindness Pledge and what they need to know to live the tenets of the pledge.

When the Kindness Initiative begins, students are at the "I" stage. They are a collection of individuals, each with his or her own set of personal needs, inclinations, and desires. Their initial concerns are for their personal safety: Will I be okay in this space? What will the teacher ask of me? Will I have any friends? Will I be laughed at if I make a mistake? Will I be able to learn? How might I be judged by the teacher and my classmates? What are the rules? Will anyone like me?

Through the classroom lessons, the teacher guides this collection of individuals toward a group identity. During common experiences, the group creates boundaries, sets up codes of behavior, establishes norms, and builds a comfortable, workable routine. In addition, group members come to discover that their strength as a group lies in honoring individual diversity and coming to understand that at the same time they hold many things in common. Central to this goal is the Circle of Kindness meeting, a weekly meeting described more fully in the following text.

When the group arrives at the "we" stage of development, the school campus is safer, positive connections are forged among students from diverse backgrounds, bridges are built between adults and students, tensions ease, and violence decreases. Within this culture of caring, students assert their rights to a peaceful community and establish a system for resolving conflicts, asking forgiveness for offending others, and forgiving personal offenses.

Students living according to the Kindness Pledge receive recognition on a daily basis, both in classrooms and on a school-wide basis. Recognition might take the form of receiving coupons that may be redeemed for prizes, hearing their names mentioned on the school public address system, being mentioned or featured in a program created by a student media team, finding their pictures on a central bulletin board, and participating in special programs and events.

Lesson Sequences

The classroom lessons are age-appropriate for students in grades K–3 and 4–8, respectively. The lessons are presented as sequences, each with a specific purpose. Activities for students in grades K–3 include four sequences. Lessons for students in grades 4–8 include these four sequences plus a fifth, as next described.

The lesson sequences are briefly outlined as follows; more detailed information about them appears in the introduction to Part 2.

Sequence 1: Basic Practices for Building a Community

This sequence creates the basic system of boundaries for a safe classroom. Teacher and students work together to create the norms the community will honor.

Sequence 2: Who We Are

Lessons in this sequence enable students to discover their own unique gifts and to accept others' talents and backgrounds.

Sequence 3: Circle of Kindness Meetings

In this sequence, classes divide into small groups and, with the help of adult leaders, establish a weekly ongoing meeting. The predictable agenda of the Circle of Kindness meeting permits students to feel safe and speak freely. That agenda is as follows:

1. Opening ritual
2. Checking in with feelings
3. Clearing a conflict, asking for forgiveness
4. Closing ritual
5. Kindness Pledge activity

Once students have mastered the agenda, they participate in a Kindness Pledge activity from Sequence 4. The meetings continue with the remaining activities from that sequence and with related activities from other sources, if desired.

Sequence 4: Living the Kindness Pledge

The lessons in this sequence reinforce commitment to living the tenets of the Kindness Pledge. In this way, students support one another's efforts to apply these values in their lives.

Sequence 5: Kindness Dilemmas

This sequence, for students in grades 4–8 only, includes five dilemmas, stories that allow students to think through situations in which a moral choice is involved. The key question for each dilemma is, What is the kind or mature thing to do in this situation? Students also have a chance to create their own dilemma stories. Dilemma stories are excellent activities for the Circle of Kindness meetings in grades 4–8.

Kind Classrooms Lesson Schedules

For the first 3 weeks of the program, a daily period to focus on program content is required. After that initial immersion, one period a week is necessary to maintain momentum and foster new skills. Tables 2 and 3 suggest lesson schedules for grades K–3 and 4–8, respectively.

Some lessons included in one age group can be used with the other, depending on the abilities of your students. For this reason, you may want to look at both schedules and select activities that best fit your group. Feel free to invent your own or include appropriate activities from other sources.

TABLE 2

Kind Classrooms Lesson Schedule: Grades K–3

SEQUENCE 1 Basic Practices for Building a Community

Week 1

Purpose

To establish basic systems, practices, norms, and rules of a community of kindness

Monday	Tuesday	Wednesday	Thursday	Friday
1.1 What Is Kindness? Using a Kindness Log	1.2 Three Basic Rules	1.3 Learning the Kindness Pledge	1.4 Doing My Best	1.5 Mail Pouches

SEQUENCE 2 Who We Are

Week 2

Purpose

To discover and honor the differences and similarities among students

Monday	Tuesday	Wednesday	Thursday	Friday
2.1 Trains	2.2 Power Circle	2.3 Card Villages	2.4 Class Quilt	2.5 Class Flag

SEQUENCE 3 Circle of Kindness Meetings

Week 3

Purpose

To establish the rituals of the Circle of Kindness meeting, a weekly small-group discussion

Monday	Tuesday	Wednesday	Thursday	Friday
3.1 Creating an Opening Ritual	3.2 Checking In with Feelings	3.3 Clearing a Conflict, Asking for Forgiveness	3.4 Creating a Closing Ritual	3.5 Kindness Pledge Activity (Lesson 4.1)

SEQUENCE 4   Living the Kindness Pledge

Weeks 4–10

Purpose

To promote students' understanding and acceptance of the tenets of the Kindness Pledge

	Week 4	**Week 5**	**Week 6**
4.1 Seeking the Positive (con-ducted during Lesson 3.5)	4.2 Putting Down Put-Downs	4.3 Honoring our Differences, Discovering our Similari-ties	4.4 Healing Our Hurts

	Week 7	**Week 8**	**Week 9**	**Week 10**
	4.5 Listening to One Another	4.6 Honoring Heroes	4.7 Reaching Higher for Success	4.8 Living Our Dreams

Note: From this point on, weekly Circle of Kindness meetings may continue with activities from other recommended sources (see page 58 and the list of resources at the back of this book).

TABLE 3

Kind Classrooms Lesson Schedule: Grades 4–8

SEQUENCE 1   Basic Practices for Building a Community

Week 1

Purpose

To establish basic systems, practices, norms, and rules of a community of kindness

Monday	*Tuesday*	*Wednesday*	*Thursday*	*Friday*
1.1 What Is Kindness? Using a Kindness Log	1.2 Three Basic Rules	1.3 Learning the Kindness Pledge	1.4 Building Integrity	1.5 A Code of Ethics

SEQUENCE 2   Who We Are

Week 2

Purpose

To discover and honor the differences and similarities among students

Monday	*Tuesday*	*Wednesday*	*Thursday*	*Friday*
2.1 My Cultures	2.2 A Collage of My Culture	2.3 Character Cards	2.4 Power Circle	2.5 Paper Beams

SEQUENCE 3   Circle of Kindness Meetings

Week 3

Purpose

To establish the rituals of the Circle of Kindness meeting, a weekly small-group discussion

Monday	*Tuesday*	*Wednesday*	*Thursday*	*Friday*
3.1 Creating an Opening Ritual	3.2 Checking In with Feelings	3.3 Clearing a Conflict, Asking for Forgiveness	3.4 Creating a Closing Ritual	3.5 Kindness Pledge Activity (Lesson 4.1)

SEQUENCE 4 Living the Kindness Pledge

Weeks 4–10

Purpose

To promote students' understanding and acceptance of the tenets of the Kindness Pledge

	Week 4 4.1 Seeking the Positive (*conducted during Lesson 3.5*)	**Week 5** 4.3 Honoring Our Differences, Discovering Our Similarities	**Week 6** 4.4 Healing Our Hurts
	Week 7 4.5 Listening to One Another	**Week 8** 4.6 Honoring Heroes	**Week 9** 4.7 Reaching Higher for Success
		Week 10 4.8 Living Our Dreams	

SEQUENCE 5 Kindness Dilemmas

Weeks 11–16

Purpose

To encourage students to experience mature decision making in a situation involving moral choice

Week 11 5.1 Jack's Dilemma	**Week 12** 5.2 Maria's Dilemma	**Week 13** 5.3 Alicia's Dilemma	**Week 14** 5.4 Takisha's Dilemma
Week 15 5.5 Roberto's Dilemma	**Week 16** 5.6 Creating Kindness Dilemmas		

Note: From this point on, weekly Circle of Kindness meetings may continue with activities from other recommended sources (see page 58 and the list of resources at the back of this book).

PART I

Kind Schools

*Peace between countries must rest on the solid
foundation of love between individuals.*

—Mahatma Gandhi

As DISCUSSED IN THE INTRODUCTION, this program has two main aspects: kind schools and kind classrooms. Each aspect supports the other. In the classroom lessons, students have the opportunity to acquire the specific skills they need to live peacefully and perform kind acts. The schoolwide activities establish a school climate in which kindness is honored and negative and violent actions are discouraged.

The heart of the schoolwide approach is the Kindness Initiative Task Force, made up of teachers and other school staff, students, and community members, including parents. This group manages and monitors the program, choosing from among a number of program components to create their own unique, site-based initiative. The task force also coordinates the initiative's activities with programs already in place in the school.

Briefly, the steps in establishing the task force are as follows:

1. Select a member from the school staff and faculty member as chair. To establish a program that will continue over time, some schools select a chairperson and an assistant who will chair the task force the following year. A member of the task force is then chosen to assist that chairperson, and the former chairperson mentors the new one. In this way, leadership revolves.

2. Select representatives from the faculty and staff, students, and community. A task force of 8 to 12 members works best. (Details of this selection process appear in Activities 1, 2, and 3.)

3. Schedule and attend an initial organizing meeting. The representatives set up the meeting schedule and begin discussing the program components they wish to include. Members of the task force may need to meet weekly as they begin their work but generally meet monthly once the program is in place.

As shown in Table 4, the task force has responsibility for seven items. The task force may choose to delegate the remaining items to action groups—groups of five or six members from the various constituent groups (faculty, students, and so forth).

WORK OF THE TASK FORCE

Selecting Staff and Faculty, Student, and Community Task Force Members

As described, the Kindness Initiative requires representatives from various groups. Together, they compose the Kindness Initiative Task Force. Activities 1, 2, and 3 offer guidelines in selecting staff and faculty, student, and community task force members.

Creating a Vision

It is important that each school create a campaign based on its particular needs and resources. In doing so, the task force drafts

TABLE 4

Schoolwide Activities

Task Force

Activity 1: Selecting Staff and Faculty Task Force Members

Activity 2: Selecting Student Task Force Members

Activity 3: Selecting Community Task Force Members

Activity 4: Creating a Vision

Activity 5: Choosing Program Components

Activity 6: Maintaining a Calendar of Events

Activity 7: Establishing Action Groups

Task Force or Action Group

Activity 8: Action-Group Planning

Activity 9: Creating Posters and Signs

Activity 10: Organizing a Kickoff Event

Activity 11: Organizing Five Days of Kindness

Activity 12: Organizing Quarterly Events

Activity 13: Using Kindness Boxes and Notes

Activity 14: Using Kindness Coupons

Activity 15: Establishing Kind Buddies Connections

Activity 16: Establishing a Study Buddies program

Activity 17: Creating a Student Service Team

Activity 18: Creating a Student Media Team

Activity 19: Identifying Guest Speakers

Activity 20: Creating a Group of Student Speakers

a mission statement to focus its work. In some schools, the task force invites students to create a cartoon character to appear on all posters and publications or to devise an original logo and motto. Contests to create original graphics and slogans add excitement to the campaign. Activity 4 includes suggestions for writing a mission statement, choosing a program name and graphic, and establishing specific, measurable program objectives.

Choosing Program Components

Not all of the campaign components described will be appropriate for every program. The task force evaluates each program component, examines policies and procedures already in place, analyzes specific needs at their site, and selects the components that will best promote kindness in their own school program.

Activity 5 lists the program components from which the task force may choose.

Maintaining a Calendar of Events

A central calendar is essential to keep program events from conflicting with one another throughout the year. The task force can note whether there are too many events within a given period of time, when events might interfere with other schoolwide programs (for instance, sports events or testing), and when even good ideas might be kept for another year. Public versions of the calendar will need to be updated throughout the year. Activity 6 describes steps in maintaining the calendar.

Establishing Action Groups

Although the task force makes sure all the work of the initiative gets done, smaller action groups often form to carry out specific projects. Members of the task force determine which responsibilities they want and need to take on themselves and which are best performed by action groups. Because action groups may include other members of the school and outside community, they broaden the scope of the initiative. Activity 7 includes suggestions for establishing action groups and identifying projects they may undertake.

WORK OF ACTION GROUPS

Action-Group Planning

Once action groups have been formed, they take on responsibility for specific projects assigned by the task force. An action planning form structures their work by including spaces to give a project description and list steps in the process, deadlines, and individuals responsible for specific components. Activity 8 gives teams instructions for constructing a solid action plan.

Creating Posters and Signs

Most schools create posters and signs to remind staff and students of the values promoted by the campaign. These include representations of the entire Kindness Pledge, the individual tenets of the pledge, and the Three Basic Rules. Activity 9 gives suggestions for involving students in the process.

Creating Kindness Initiative Events

To maintain students' interest and program momentum, many schools set up special events several times during the year. A special event might be as simple as showing the student body a film that projects positive values, followed by small-group discussion, or as complicated as a retreat or an all-school field day. Small daily events might include viewing a short film reflecting the value of kindness or presenting a 10-minute skit or sing-a-long. Three specific types of events are as follows:

Kick-off event: Held early in the school year, this is a dramatic, high-energy event to introduce the Kindness Initiative. (See Activity 10.)

Five days of kindness: Following the kick-off event, schools create a short daily event for the subsequent four days. These events emphasize the importance of the Kindness Initiative and set the stage for future events. (See Activity 11.)

Quarterly events: A major event is planned for each quarter (or at other major mileposts). Examples include a field trip, a fair, or a day of noncompetitive games devoted to the value of kindness. (See Activity 12.)

Using Kindness Boxes and Notes

Located around the school, Kindness Boxes are places for students to drop Kindness Notes that describe the kind acts they observe. Each box is placed in a central location, along with a supply of Kindness Notes. Members of the task force or action group collect and read these notes on a weekly basis. Students who have been "caught being kind" receive Kindness Coupons, are invited to special events during the year, and are recognized in other ways on a schoolwide basis. Activity 13 explains how to construct and use Kindness Boxes and Kindness Notes.

Using Kindness Coupons

Students who receive Kindness Notes receive Kindness Coupons and other rewards. Other students and staff can also be awarded Kindness Coupons for their notable acts of kindness. Kindness Coupons may be redeemed at a student "store" and, if desired, traded for small purchases at participating local businesses. Instructions for creating and using Kindness Coupons appear in Activity 14.

Establishing Kind Buddies Connections

The Kind Buddies Connection establishes relationships between older and younger students, to their mutual benefit. Every child in the school has a buddy. Buddies connect at special buddy programs—game days, field days, films, speakers—held four or five times a year, either separately or combined with quarterly events. Activity 15 describes the Kind Buddies Connection in more detail.

Establishing a Study Buddies Program

Some schools establish a team of seventh and eighth graders who help students in the lower grades with their schoolwork. Teachers recommend older students to serve as tutors and provide information about schoolwork on which the younger students need assistance. The formation of the Study Buddies program is described in Activity 16.

Creating a Student Service Team

Some schools team a faculty adviser with a group of older students who are willing to perform acts of service in the school throughout the year. Service acts might involve forming a team of ushers and cleanup groups for a special event, helping a staff member with a special project, setting up chairs for a speaker, and various other acts of service in the community. Activity 17 outlines procedures for establishing this type of service team.

Creating a Student Media Team

Some schools create a media team composed of students who, with the help of a faculty adviser, produce a weekly audio or audiovisual program on the theme of kindness. Possible programs include an interview with students who have been named in Kindness Notes and a skit involving students from various grade levels on the topic of kindness. Activity 18 provides additional information about the Student Media Team.

Identifying Guest Speakers

Every community has people who are making a difference, choosing lifestyles that center on service, and giving their time and talent to the community. Guest speakers from the community link the school's Kindness Initiative with students' lives outside the school. Possible speakers include police and fire fighters, members of community service clubs, and representatives of charity organizations. Activity 19 makes suggestions for identifying speakers from the community.

Creating a Group of Student Speakers

Some schools also find it helpful to create a team of staff and students who are willing and available to speak to groups in the community about the Kindness Initiative. Groups interested in hearing such presentations include local businesses, service agencies, and the media. Activity 20 spells out procedures for choosing student speakers and includes some of the topics that can be included in a presentation.

Selecting Staff and Faculty Task Force Members

Purpose ▷ To attract a group of highly committed staff and faculty to the task force

Materials ▷ Copies of the Staff and Faculty Recommendation Form

Preparation ▷ Schedule a presentation for staff and faculty to present the principles of the Kindness Initiative and responsibilities of the task force.

Directions
1. Describe the Kindness Initiative and the work of the task force. Point out the responsibilities of the members of the task force, including the following:
   ▷ Attending all meetings
   ▷ Recruiting other staff members for special projects
   ▷ Heading action groups
   ▷ Supporting the program throughout the school

2. Distribute the Staff and Faculty Recommendation Forms. Ask staff and faculty to recommend those they believe would be effective in serving on the task force or in leading action groups.

3. Using additional copies of the Staff and Faculty Recommendation Form, survey students in the sixth, seventh, and eighth grades as to which teachers are, in their opinion, the most influential and communicate the best with students.

4. Compare the list of staff and faculty named most often with the list generated by students.

5. Invite several teachers and staff members whose names appear on both lists to work on the task force.

6. Keep the combined list, and invite remaining staff and faculty to head or work on action groups.

Staff and Faculty Recommendation Form

I recommend the following staff or faculty members to work
on the Kindness Initiative Task Force:

1. _____

2. _____

3. _____

4. _____

5. _____

Staff and Faculty Recommendation Form

I recommend the following staff or faculty members to work
on the Kindness Initiative Task Force:

1. _____

2. _____

3. _____

4. _____

5. _____

Selecting Student Task Force Members

Purpose ▷ To create a group of older students committed to providing the task force with student input

Materials ▷ Copies of the Student Application and Student Recommendation Form

Preparation ▷ Schedule an assembly or separate meetings for students at the upper grade levels to introduce students to the Kindness Initiative and the work of the task force. (In a K–8 school, these would be sixth, seventh, and eighth graders; in a K–5 school, students would be fifth graders.)

Directions
1. Describe the Kindness Initiative and the work of the Kindness Initiative Task Force.

2. Distribute the Student Applications. Point out the responsibilities of a student member of the task force, as described on the application.

3. Distribute the Student Recommendation Forms. Ask students to select three classmates they could support as members of the task force.

4. Ask students to apply for a position on the task force if they are willing to fulfill the responsibilities.

5. Compare the recommendations and applications. Select two students from each grade level to serve on the task force. Keep the recommendation forms and applications to use when selecting other students to work in action groups or on specific tasks.

Student Application

Name _____ **Date** _____ **Class or homeroom** _____

Put a check mark beside each statement if you agree.

❑ I agree to attend all planning meetings.

❑ I agree to be part of one or more action groups and to attend their planning meetings and events.

❑ I agree to recruit other students to participate on action groups and at events.

❑ I agree to maintain my grade-point average. I understand that if my grades go down I may be asked to leave the Kindness Initiative Task Force and any action groups to which I belong.

❑ I agree to support the Kindness Initiative actively and positively throughout the school and to participate in its events.

A teacher or other staff person who knows me and will recommend me is

_____.

Student Application

Name _____ **Date** _____ **Class or homeroom** _____

Put a check mark beside each statement if you agree.

❑ I agree to attend all planning meetings.

❑ I agree to be part of one or more action groups and to attend their planning meetings and events.

❑ I agree to recruit other students to participate on action groups and at events.

❑ I agree to maintain my grade-point average. I understand that if my grades go down I may be asked to leave the Kindness Initiative Task Force and any action groups to which I belong.

❑ I agree to support the Kindness Initiative actively and positively throughout the school and to participate in its events.

A teacher or other staff person who knows me and will recommend me is

_____.

Student Recommendation Form

I recommend the following students as members of the Kindness Initiative Task Force:

1. _____

2. _____

3. _____

Student Recommendation Form

I recommend the following students as members of the Kindness Initiative Task Force:

1. _____

2. _____

3. _____

Student Recommendation Form

I recommend the following students as members of the Kindness Initiative Task Force:

1. _____

2. _____

3. _____

Student Recommendation Form

I recommend the following students as members of the Kindness Initiative Task Force:

1. _____

2. _____

3. _____

Selecting Community Task Force Members

Purpose ▷ To select active and influential members of the community to serve on the task force

Materials ▷ Access to telephones

Preparation ▷ Identify four or five people who are willing to make a number of telephone calls.

Directions 1. As a group, brainstorm the names of a number of influential community members.

2. Call each of the selected individuals, asking them to name three to five community members they believe would work well on the task force.

3. Call each of the individuals these people named; ask each of them to name three to five additional people.

4. Compare the lists formed. Select those people appearing on both lists as candidates for membership on the task force.

5. Invite several members of the community to serve, pointing out the responsibilities of membership:

   ▷ Attending all meetings

   ▷ Recruiting other community members for special projects

   ▷ Heading action groups

   ▷ Supporting the program throughout the community

Creating a Vision

Purpose ▷ To create a site-based vision to inform the development of the school's Kindness Initiative

Materials ▷ Materials as needed for each item

Preparation ▷ Schedule a meeting of the task force.

Directions

Program Name

Brainstorm and select an appropriate name for the program, or set up a contest among the students to name the program. If you set up a contest, follow these steps:

1. Announce the contest to the student body.
2. Set a deadline for submissions.
3. Ask the task force to select three to five submissions.
4. Let the student body vote on the name.
5. Reward the winner with 10 Kindness Coupons (see Activity 14).

Program Slogan

Create a slogan for the program, or set up a contest among the students using steps similar to the ones just listed. Examples include "It's Cool to be Kind" and "Kindness Counts."

Program Graphic

Create a graphic to symbolize the program, or set up a contest among the students using steps like those given for program name and slogan.

Program Mission

As a group, attempt to describe in one or two sentences the mission of your program. For example:

It is the mission of the Kindness Initiative to create a school environment that encourages kind and compassionate treatment of all students and staff, promotes personal integrity and leadership in members of the school community, and encourages the performance of positive actions on the behalf of others.

Program Objectives

Create a set of specific objectives you seek to reach with your program. For example:

▷ To identify 100 acts of kindness on campus in one semester

▷ To increase student involvement in schoolwide projects

▷ To lower the number of acts of violence and bullying by 50 percent by the end of the year

▷ To generate 10 positive stories about the school, staff, and students in local media (TV, radio, newspaper)

▷ To recognize five graduates who have made positive contributions to the community

▷ To unite all parts of the campus—including parent groups, athletic teams and coaches, community support groups, and so forth—in the planning and work of the initiative

Make sure to review these objectives at meetings of the task force to give the program a definite direction and to assess progress.

Choosing Program Components

Purpose	▷ To determine the scope and specific components of the program
Materials	▷ Copies of the Program Components list
Preparation	▷ Schedule a meeting of the task force.
Directions	*Use the list on the next page to discuss and determine the scope of your program. Feel free to add any site-specific ideas you wish.*

Program Components

❏ **Task Force:** A group of students, teachers, staff, and community members meeting regularly to review process and make plans

❏ **Program Vision:** Involving creation of a slogan and/or graphic, development of a mission statement, and identification of measurable objectives

❏ **Calendar:** Updated regularly to list program events over the school year

❏ **Action Groups:** Groups that take on special projects, composed of five or six individuals from the campaign's constituents (staff, students, community members)

❏ **Posters and Signs:** Located throughout the school to remind students of the Kindness Pledge and the Three Basic Rules.

❏ **Events:** Designed to promote kind behaviors:
    ❏ Kick-off event
    ❏ Five days of kindness
    ❏ Quarterly events
    ❏ Other events

❏ **Kindness Boxes:** Located around the school, in which students and staff can anonymously put notes reporting kinds acts

❏ **Kindness Coupons:** Coupons that students "caught being kind" receive, with which they can purchase small items from a school store or local participating businesses

❏ **Kind Buddies Connections:** A schoolwide buddy program in which older and younger students are paired in order to connect on a regular basis at special buddy events

❏ **Study Buddies:** Pairs of older and younger students, in which the older students help the younger students with their schoolwork on a regular basis

❏ **Student Service Team:** A group of students who can be called on to perform acts of service throughout the year (ushering, cleanup, special projects, and the like)

❏ **Student Media Team:** A group of students who design audio or audiovisual productions promoting kindness in the school

❏ **Guest Speakers:** Community members who are promoting positive change in the community and are willing to speak with students

❏ **Student Speakers:** A group of students who are willing to speak to local community groups about the program

Maintaining a Calendar of Events

Purpose ▷ To create and maintain a central calendar so everyone is informed of upcoming Kindness Initiative events

Materials ▷ A large calendar on which information can be readily updated, posted in a central location. Specific materials depend on the school's choice: Some schools purchase a large desk calendar. Others devote an entire bulletin board to Kindness Initiative information.

Preparation ▷ Schedule a meeting of the task force.

Directions

1. Designate a single member of the task force to create and manage the calendar. Make sure that everyone on the task force and on action groups knows to submit event dates to this person.

2. Empower the calendar person to negotiate if groups propose the same date for an event or if program events conflict with other scheduled school activities.

3. Ask the calendar person to create weekly and monthly updates. A weekly list of events should be circulated to faculty and staff. A monthly calendar of events should be available to all staff, students, and interested members of the community.

Establishing Action Groups

Purpose ▷ To identify projects that need small-group planning and create action groups to accomplish them

Materials ▷ Program Components list (from Activity 5)

▷ A Project Description Form for each proposed project

Preparation ▷ Schedule a meeting of the task force. Assemble the lists of students and adults who do not serve on the task force but who have expressed interest in working with the campaign (from Activities 1 through 3).

Directions
1. Review the program components you chose in Activity 5, and determine those suited to small-group planning and operation.
2. Select an adult and student leader for each action group. Adult and student leaders then select group members.
3. Discuss and determine a deadline for project completion.
4. Suggest appropriate times for the team to report to the task force on progress.
5. Give action-team leaders a completed copy of the Project Description Form.

Project Description Form

Project name _____ **Date** _____

Adult group leader _____

Student group leader _____

Project description _____

_____

_____

_____

_____

_____

_____

Progress report dates

_____ _____ _____ _____

Proposed date of completion _____

Comments _____

_____

_____

_____

Action-Group Planning

Purpose ▷ To create an action plan for each proposed program event or activity

Materials ▷ A copy of the Action-Planning Form for each proposed project

Preparation ▷ Schedule a meeting of the action group.

Directions 1. In the small group, work together to develop a plan of action. Use the following guidelines to complete the form:

Project: Identify the project by name or brief description.

Group leaders: Name the adult and student overseeing the entire project.

Group members: Name those supporting and working on the project.

Steps: Describe every step necessary to complete the project.

Who: Name person responsible for each step.

When: Note the date that the step must be completed.

Comments: Include any special information or notes.

2. Check the following:

Have you listed all the steps necessary to complete the project?

Do you have a person responsible for each step?

Are the due dates for step completion reasonable?

Do you need anyone's help or support who is not in the group?

From whom do you need to get approval (principal, assistant principal, other)?

When will the action group meet again?

Action-Planning Form

Project name _____ **Date** _____

Group leaders _____

Group members _____

Steps	Who?	When?

1. _____

   _____

2. _____

   _____

3. _____

   _____

4. _____

   _____

5. _____

   _____

Target completion date _____

Comments _____

_____

_____

_____

Creating Posters and Signs

Purpose   ▷   To create signs to be posted around the school to remind staff and students of the nine tenets of the Kindness Pledge and the Three Basic Rules

Materials   ▷   Poster board, markers, construction paper, and other art supplies

▷   Copies of the Kindness Pledge and Three Basic Rules (see Appendix C)

Preparation   ▷   Create a group of teachers and students to select five finalists from each of the grades.

Directions   *The following instructions refer to the Kindness Pledge but also apply generally to the Three Basic Rules.*

Plan 1

1. Assign one of the nine tenets of the Kindness Pledge to each grade level. (Some grades may work on more than one.)
2. Ask students at that level to make and decorate a poster illustrating the tenet.
3. Have a group of teacher and student judges select five finalists for each tenet. (Some schools elect to focus on one tenet a month. In that case, all the posters could be saved to be displayed during that month.)
4. Have the judges choose one sign for each tenet to illustrate the complete Kindness Pledge.
5. Honor the five finalists by laminating their signs and posting them in a central location (school entrance, cafeteria, outside the principal's office).
6. Honor students who participated but whose signs were not selected by posting their signs in classrooms and other areas throughout the school.
7. Give all participants Kindness Coupons (see Activity 14).

Plan 2

1. Announce to students that you will select 25 ideas for a poster illustrating all nine tenets of the Kindness Pledge. Ask students to create and submit their ideas. (Some schools decide to use all the designs rather than limiting them to 25.)
2. If you receive more than 25 designs, have a group of teacher and student judges choose from among them.

3. Take the designs chosen to a copy shop and have them enlarged and laminated.

4. Post these Kindness Pledge signs in central locations in the school.

5. Post the signs not chosen in classrooms and other areas throughout the school.

6. Give all participants Kindness Coupons.

Other Ideas

1. Have a professional sign company create banners of the separate tenets and the entire Kindness Pledge, incorporating a student-created graphic or cartoon character.

2. Ask a billboard company to create billboards of student designs and put them up around the community as a public service.

3. Ask a printing business to produce a calendar with student designs for every family to have at home.

4. Ask the local newspaper to publish the Kindness Pledge and the Three Basic Rules in the newspaper during the program's kickoff week.

Organizing a Kickoff Event

Purpose ▷ To create and stage a compelling event that will introduce the Kindness Initiative to the school community

Materials ▷ Copies of the Action-Planning Form (from Activity 8)

▷ Other materials as required by the events chosen

Preparation ▷ Schedule a meeting of the task force or action group.

Directions 1. As a group, consider the following components of the Kindness Initiative:

▷ Kindness Pledge

▷ Three Basic Rules

▷ Kindness Boxes

▷ Kindness Coupons

2. Brainstorm plans to motivate the students to embrace the program. Some suggestions follow.

School 1

One school held an all-school assembly. A local DJ hosted the hour-long event. Copies of the Kindness Pledge were handed out, and a large version was projected on a screen behind the stage.

During the assembly, the school band and cheerleaders performed and danced. The music director selected upbeat music, and the cheerleaders adapted some cheers to perform with the assembly.

The principal announced that the Kindness Initiative would last all year and described some of its schoolwide components and activities. All rose and recited the Kindness Pledge, and everyone received a Kindness Coupon.

School 2

At another school, the principal declared a "Random Acts of Kindness Day." Throughout the morning, a select group of teachers and students performed acts of kindness for other teachers and students (for instance, cleaning up specific school areas, carrying lunch trays, serving drinks and desserts at lunch).

In an afternoon assembly, the principal enthusiastically described the year-long initiative and invited everyone to participate. The principal's remarks were followed by fun games and events. In this school, the entire event was kept a surprise by the principal, task force, and other staff.

3. Use an Action-Planning Form to outline the steps in the kick-off event.

4. Announce the kickoff event to staff and faculty, and add it to the calendar.

5. Send a press release describing the campaign and the kickoff event to local media.

6. Hold the kickoff event as planned.

Organizing Five Days of Kindness

Purpose   ▷ To emphasize the school's commitment to the Kindness Initiative

Materials   ▷ Copies of the Action-Planning Form (from Activity 8)

▷ Other materials as required for the events chosen

Preparation   ▷ Schedule a meeting of the task force or action group.

Directions   1. As a group, brainstorm a series of short events to follow the Kindness Initiative's kickoff. Each daily event should be fun but brief—no longer than 20 to 30 minutes. Here are some ideas for schoolwide assemblies:

> If you did not have a motivational speaker at your kickoff event, invite an enthusiastic and inspiring speaker from the community to address the students.

> Ask each grade level to create and perform a cheer. Then, at a schoolwide assembly, have each grade level stand and give their cheer. Moving from group to group keeps the entire assembly energized.

> Ask students from the same grade level to create skits for each of the tenets of the Kindness Pledge. Have the students perform their skits for the school.

> Ask a group of creative students to create a rap or theme song, then teach it to the assembly. (Songs with movement are especially good—clap hands, slap thighs, snap fingers, stand up, sit down, and so forth). Each grade level can then perform the rap or song for the entire assembly.

> Ask the school librarian to suggest short stories or films on the subject of kindness. Stories may be read aloud and films shown, then followed by discussion. (If a story is to be read, be sure the reader is highly animated and can engage large groups.)

> Ask a local singer or storyteller who performs for children to share songs or stories on the theme of kindness.

2. Use an Action-Planning Form to outline the steps in each event.

3. Contact and schedule any speakers or performers.

4. Add these special activities to the central calendar. Make sure to inform all faculty and staff that each day a short special program will be held.

Organizing Quarterly Events

Purpose ▷ To create larger events to keep students motivated to partici-pate in the Kindness Initiative

Materials ▷ Copies of the Action-Planning Form (from Activity 8)

▷ Materials as required for the events chosen

Preparation ▷ Schedule a meeting of the task force or action group.

Directions 1. As a task force or action group, select four dates spaced throughout the year on which to conduct full-day activities.

2. Brainstorm possible full-day events. For example:

One school held a kindness fair by asking local communi-ty and student groups to set up displays of their service programs. Students toured the displays, then attended an assembly in which people from the various groups described their programs.

Another school brought in a trainer who specialized in noncompetitive sports and games. The trainer supervised a day of fun activities in the school gym for each grade level.

A series of activity stations were set up at another school. In the morning, small groups of students from various grade levels visited each station for a 20-minute activity that emphasized working together. Parents and commu-nity members led the groups and assisted at the stations. In the afternoon, a group of high school outreach stu-dents put on an assembly of skits and cheers.

One school kept a list of people in the community who performed kind acts that were written up in the newspa-per or reported on radio and TV. They also asked each local community agency to nominate people they believed made the community better through their acts of kindness. The school designed an award to give and held an awards assembly to honor these citizens.

Several schools selected 80 to 100 students for a special day of activities led by a local activities trainer; others took youths to a local "ropes course" for a day of activi-ties. In many communities, the YMCA or YWCA or adventure-experience groups supervise such activities.

Other schools scheduled a day of field trips to local agen-cies devoted to service for others (for example, fire and police stations, food banks, missions, soup kitchens, and churches).

3. Use an Action-Planning Form to detail each event.

4. Select students who have demonstrated a pattern of kindness to be involved in planning these special events. Make sure to select a new group of students for each new event.

Using Kindness Boxes and Notes

Purpose   ▷ To identify acts of kindness throughout the school

Materials   ▷ Several medium-sized boxes

▷ Art supplies

▷ Copies of the Kindness Note

Preparation   ▷ Schedule a meeting of the task force or action group.

Directions   1. Ask students from each grade level to label and decorate one or more Kindness Boxes. Each box should have a slot on the top where Kindness Notes may be inserted.

2. Establish several locations for the boxes (outside the school office, cafeteria, library, anywhere students congregate).

3. Notify staff and students that whenever they see someone performing an act of kindness, they may complete a Kindness Note and drop it in the box. Explain that anyone can use the box: Students can honor students or adults, and adults can honor students or other adults. Also explain that you will be acknowledging the performers of kind acts and, if they wish to include their names, the reporters of those events.

4. Make sure to keep a supply of Kindness Notes at each box.

5. Empty and review the contents of the Kindness Boxes once a week.

6. Mention selected kind acts weekly during the morning announcements or in productions of the Student Media Team, if you have established one (see Activity 18).

7. Award Kindness Coupons (described in Activity 14) to students who have performed or reported kind acts.

8. Remind students from time to time to use the boxes.

Kindness Note

Name (if you wish to give it) _____

Today's date _____

Where did the act occur? _____

When did the act occur? Date _____ Time _____

Describe what happened. (Who performed the act? What was the result?)

_____

_____

_____

Kindness Note

Name (if you wish to give it) _____

Today's date _____

Where did the act occur? _____

When did the act occur? Date _____ Time _____

Describe what happened. (Who performed the act? What was the result?)

_____

_____

_____

Using Kindness Coupons

Purpose   ▷ To reward students who perform kind acts and the students who recognize them

Materials   ▷ Small items with which to stock a school store (pencils, erasers, toys from a fast-food chain, gum, and so on)

▷ Copies of the Kindness Coupon

Preparation   ▷ Establish and stock a school store at which students may redeem their coupons.

Directions   1. Brainstorm possible sponsors who could either contribute directly to the purchase of small items or allow students to exchange Kindness Coupons at their stores.

2. Contact and compile a list of local sponsors who accept the invitation to participate in the coupon exchange. Let potential sponsors know that each coupon will be worth 50 cents to a dollar. (Most businesses offer drinks or candy bars for redemption.)

3. Make the coupons available to staff and faculty. A sample follows; the text of your coupon(s) may vary.

 KINDNESS COUPON

Thank you for being kind.

You may exchange this coupon for an item in the school store or at a store on the Kindness Initiative's sponsor list.

Thanks again for your thoughtfulness!

---

4. Encourage staff and faculty to distribute the coupons to any students who demonstrate kind acts. (They should strive to give out at least two per day.)

5. Notify students of the availability of coupons and the ways they can be redeemed (school store or local businesses). Encourage students to give their coupons to other students who appear to need a kind act.

Establishing Kind Buddies Connections

Purpose ▷ To create a more positive climate throughout the school by promoting a bond between older and younger students

Materials ▷ Materials as needed for the events chosen

Preparation ▷ Schedule a meeting of the task force or action group.

▷ Recruit a faculty adviser to supervise the project.

Directions 1. Pair each older student with at least one younger buddy. (More mature older buddies can have two buddies.) In a K–8 school, pairing students in the following way allows the buddy relationships to grow over time:

▷ Fifth graders pair with kindergartners and first graders.

▷ Sixth graders pair with second graders.

▷ Seventh graders pair with third graders.

▷ Eighth graders pair with fourth graders.

A significant age difference between buddies is important. Pairings for a K–5 school could be as follows:

▷ Third graders pair with kindergartners.

▷ Fourth graders pair with first graders.

▷ Fifth graders pair with second graders.

2. Brainstorm four or five buddy events that are fun and take no longer than 45 minutes. For example:

Films: Show an exciting children's film that all age groups can enjoy.

Buddy lunches: One grade takes the other to lunch at school.

Board games: Both buddies bring a game. (Make sure both games are played.)

Guest speakers: Older buddies escort younger ones to the location of the guest speaker.

Field day: A sequence of fun games and sports activities. (Follow with a buddy picnic.)

Usually, older students escort their younger buddies to special events, sit with them, and give them lots of attention. Students on the task force or in action groups often have great ideas!

3. Have the faculty adviser oversee each event. Periodically, the action group can interview the buddies to see how relationships are developing.

Establishing a Study Buddies Program

Purpose   ▷ To provide an opportunity for older students to tutor and help younger students, to their mutual benefit

Materials   ▷ Copies of the Study Buddies Application

Preparation   ▷ Schedule a meeting of the task force or action group.

▷ Recruit a faculty adviser to supervise the project.

▷ Determine a central area (for example, a classroom or the library) in which buddies may work.

Directions   1. For K–8 schools, describe the program to students in grades 7 and 8. Include these ideas:

▷ Seventh and eighth graders form a team of tutors who help younger students at a scheduled time (during the lunch hour, a study period, or after school).

▷ Study buddies review concepts suggested by teachers, read with the younger students, and help them with assignments or worksheets.

In K–5 schools, describe the program to fifth graders. Fifth graders can tutor students in grades K–3. (Fourth graders may be too close in age to fifth graders to be tutored by them.)

2. Copy and distribute the Study Buddies Applications to interested students in the upper grades.

3. Select approximately 25 students to get started as tutors. (You may need to recruit more later.)

4. Ask teachers of the various grades to recommend younger students for tutoring.

5. Pair the older students with the younger ones so the pairs work together for at least a semester.

6. Have the faculty adviser supervise the program and make any necessary changes.

Study Buddies Application

Name _____ **Date** _____ **Class or homeroom** _____

Put a check mark in the box beside each statement if you agree.

❏ I agree to attend all tutoring sessions.

❏ I agree to be attentive to the student I am tutoring.

❏ I agree to recruit other students if needed.

❏ I agree to maintain my grade-point average. I understand that if my grades go down I may be asked to leave the Study Buddies program.

❏ I agree to support the Kindness Initiative actively and positively throughout the school and to participate in its events.

A teacher or staff person who knows me and will recommend me is

_____.

Study Buddies Application

Name _____ **Date** _____ **Class or homeroom** _____

Put a check mark in the box beside each statement if you agree.

❏ I agree to attend all tutoring sessions.

❏ I agree to be attentive to the student I am tutoring.

❏ I agree to recruit other students if needed.

❏ I agree to maintain my grade-point average. I understand that if my grades go down I may be asked to leave the Study Buddies program.

❏ I agree to support the Kindness Initiative actively and positively throughout the school and to participate in its events.

A teacher or staff person who knows me and will recommend me is

_____.

Cultivating Kindness in School: Activities That Promote Integrity, Respect, and Compassion in Elementary and Middle School Students.
© 2004 by Ric Stuecker. Champaign, IL: Research Press. (800) 519–2707.

Creating a Student Service Team

Purpose ▷ To create a team of students to work at special events and to help staff as needs arise

Materials ▷ Copies of the Student Service Team Application

Preparation ▷ Schedule a meeting of the task force or action group.

▷ Recruit a faculty adviser to supervise the project.

Directions 1. Explain the purpose of the Student Service Team to students: To help out with the school's special programs and provide other assistance in support of the Kindness Initiative.

2. Give students who express interest a copy of the Student Service Team Application. Have these students fill out and return the application.

3. From the list of volunteers, select a team of 15 to 20 students.

4. As need arises, ask students to help set up for special events, act as ushers, help with cleanup, and perform other services.

5. Have the faculty adviser supervise the team's efforts.

Student Service Team Application

Name _____ **Date** _____ **Class or homeroom** _____

Put a check mark in the box beside each statement if you agree.

❏ I agree to be available to help staff as needed.

❏ I agree to be attentive to the task when I am working.

❏ I agree to recruit other students for the team if needed.

❏ I agree to maintain my grade-point average. I understand that if my grades go down I may be asked to leave the service team.

❏ I agree to support the Kindness Initiative actively and positively throughout the school and to participate in its events.

A teacher or staff person who knows me and will recommend me is

_____.

Student Service Team Application

Name _____ **Date** _____ **Class or homeroom** _____

Put a check mark in the box beside each statement if you agree.

❏ I agree to be available to help staff as needed.

❏ I agree to be attentive to the task when I am working.

❏ I agree to recruit other students for the team if needed.

❏ I agree to maintain my grade-point average. I understand that if my grades go down I may be asked to leave the service team.

❏ I agree to support the Kindness Initiative actively and positively throughout the school and to participate in its events.

A teacher or staff person who knows me and will recommend me is

_____.

Cultivating Kindness in School: Activities That Promote Integrity, Respect, and Compassion in Elementary and Middle School Students.
© 2004 by Ric Stuecker. Champaign, IL: Research Press. (800) 519–2707.

Creating a Student Media Team

Purpose ▷ To create a team of students who plan and create audio or audiovisual productions that support the goals of the Kindness Initiative

Materials ▷ Copies of the Student Media Team Application

▷ Access to audio and/or audiovisual recording and broadcast equipment

Preparation ▷ Schedule a meeting of the task force or action group.

▷ Recruit a faculty adviser to supervise the project.

Directions 1. Explain the purpose of the Student Media Team to students: To create a weekly audio or audiovisual program, no longer than 20 minutes, that features stories about the Kindness Initiative and includes information about other school events.

2. Distribute copies of the Student Media Team Application, and ask students who wish to participate to fill it out and return it.

3. From the group of applicants, select a team of five or six students.

4. Have the faculty adviser work with the team to plan and produce the weekly program. Each week, a different student may take the role of announcer. Here are some story ideas:

   ▷ Reports on general events on campus, the performance of various sports teams, lunch menus, and Kindness Initiative events

   ▷ Interviews with students or staff who have been named in the Kindness Box

   ▷ Interviews with people who provide community services. (Consult the list of guest speakers, if you have one—see Activity 19.)

   ▷ Skits, original stories, or the reading of a favorite short book with kindness as the theme by students from each of the grade levels

5. Record the program, then present it schoolwide through the public address or closed-circuit television system.

Student Media Team Application

Name _____ **Date** _____ **Class or homeroom** _____

Put a check mark in the box beside each statement if you agree.

❑ I agree to help create and produce a media program once a week.

❑ I agree to prepare my part of the program prior to the taping.

❑ I agree to be attentive to the task when I am working with the team.

❑ I agree to recruit other students if needed.

❑ I agree to maintain my grade-point average. I understand that if my grades go down I may be asked to leave the Student Media Team.

❑ I agree to support the Kindness Initiative actively and positively throughout the school and to participate in its events.

A teacher or staff person who knows me and will recommend me is

_____.

Student Media Team Application

Name _____ **Date** _____ **Class or homeroom** _____

Put a check mark in the box beside each statement if you agree.

❑ I agree to help create and produce a media program once a week.

❑ I agree to prepare my part of the program prior to the taping.

❑ I agree to be attentive to the task when I am working with the team.

❑ I agree to recruit other students if needed.

❑ I agree to maintain my grade-point average. I understand that if my grades go down I may be asked to leave the Student Media Team.

❑ I agree to support the Kindness Initiative actively and positively throughout the school and to participate in its events.

A teacher or staff person who knows me and will recommend me is

_____.

Identifying Guest Speakers

Purpose
▷ To identify guest speakers to address individual classes and the whole school about the work they do in service to others

Materials
▷ Access to telephones
▷ Copies of the Guest Speaker Identification Form

Preparation
▷ Schedule a meeting of the task force or action group.

Directions
1. Make a list of agencies that are likely sources of speakers. For example:
   ▷ Police department
   ▷ Fire department
   ▷ Community service agencies
   ▷ United Way
   ▷ Boy and Girl Scouts
   ▷ Charitable organizations
   ▷ Local hospitals

2. Note any local news stories that feature people you may want to ask.

3. Contact any organizations that give awards for service, and ask for a list of winners and candidates.

4. Contact each potential speaker and ask about his or her willingness and availability to speak. Fill out a Speaker Identification Form for each person who accepts.

5. Select the five speakers you think would be the most compelling for schoolwide presentations. Make sure to identify two or three alternates.

6. From the Guest Speaker Identification Forms of those not chosen for schoolwide presentations, create a list of speakers for classrooms. Suggest to teachers that they ask these speakers to address their classes (one speaker per month, if possible).

7. Schedule the speakers. Be sure to list the times on the program's calendar.

Guest Speaker Identification Form

Name of caller _____ **Date** _____

Name/affiliation of speaker _____

Why would this individual make a compelling speaker?

_____

_____

_____

Speaker's availability _____

Recommended for whole school? ❑ Classroom? ❑ Both? ❑

Guest Speaker Identification Form

Name of caller _____ **Date** _____

Name/affiliation of speaker _____

Why would this individual make a compelling speaker?

_____

_____

_____

Speaker's availability _____

Recommended for whole school? ❑ Classroom? ❑ Both? ❑

Cultivating Kindness in School: Activities That Promote Integrity, Respect, and Compassion in Elementary and Middle School Students.
© 2004 by Ric Stuecker. Champaign, IL: Research Press. (800) 519–2707.

Creating a Group of Student Speakers

Purpose ▷ To create a team of students who can speak to local groups about the work of the Kindness Initiative

Materials ▷ Copies of the Student Speakers Application

▷ Paper and access to a photocopy machine

▷ Drawing and design supplies (or publishing software, if available)

▷ Envelopes and postage

Preparation ▷ Schedule a meeting of the task force or action group.

▷ Recruit a faculty adviser to supervise the project.

Directions 1. Explain the purpose of the team to students: To establish a group of students who, with a faculty adviser, will spread the word about the Kindness Initiative. Groups of two or three students and the adviser will address local community agencies, the school board, the parent-teacher association, and the media.

2. Give interested students a copy of the Student Speakers Application.

3. From those who apply, select 8 to 10 students.

4. Create a script or outline for students to use when they appear in front of groups. Some points to include are as follows:

   ▷ The Kindness Initiative's mission statement

   ▷ Program objectives

   ▷ Examples of events and projects

   ▷ How students are personally affected by the Kindness Initiative

5. Create a one-page flyer describing the Kindness Initiative and explaining how to schedule an appearance.

6. Mail the flyer to members of the school board, the parent-teacher organization, local business groups, community service organizations, and the media.

7. Have students present their speech to groups that express interest.

Student Speakers Application

Name _____ **Date** _____ **Class or homeroom** _____

Put a check mark in the box beside each statement if you agree.

❏ I agree to help create a program format.

❏ I agree to prepare my part of the program prior to speaking.

❏ I agree to be attentive to the task when I am working with the team.

❏ I agree to recruit other students if needed.

❏ I agree to maintain my grade-point average. I understand that if my grades go down I may be asked to leave the speakers group.

❏ I agree to support the Kindness Initiative actively and positively throughout the school and to participate in its events.

A teacher or staff person who knows me and will recommend me is

_____ .

Student Speakers Application

Name _____ **Date** _____ **Class or homeroom** _____

Put a check mark in the box beside each statement if you agree.

❏ I agree to help create a program format.

❏ I agree to prepare my part of the program prior to speaking.

❏ I agree to be attentive to the task when I am working with the team.

❏ I agree to recruit other students if needed.

❏ I agree to maintain my grade-point average. I understand that if my grades go down I may be asked to leave the speakers group.

❏ I agree to support the Kindness Initiative actively and positively throughout the school and to participate in its events.

A teacher or staff person who knows me and will recommend me is

_____ .

PART 2

Kind Classrooms

We are all children of the Great Spirit—we all belong to Mother Earth. Our planet is in great trouble, and if we keep carrying old grudges and do not work together, we will die.

—Chief Seattle

THE KIND CLASSROOMS LESSONS augment the schoolwide efforts discussed in Part 1, "Kind Schools," and help classrooms become learning communities, assist teachers in implementing the three-rule management system, and give students the opportunity to learn the specific skills they need to live the tenets of the Kindness Pledge. Furthermore, each classroom establishes a weekly time to create and maintain this community, recognize individuals, develop support among the students to live the kindness skills they learn, clear up any conflicts among students, and participate in activities that further enrich the kindness program.

Four lesson sequences, next described, allow teachers to create a community of kindness in kindergarten through grade 3 classrooms. Teachers of grades 4 through 8 undertake these four lesson sequences, plus the fifth sequence listed.

Sequence 1: Basic Practices for Building a Community

This lesson sequence establishes the basic practices school communities need to function well. Teachers and students working together come to a common understanding of the Three Basic Rules they will live under during their time together. By using a Kindness Log, they discover the types and qualities of kind acts they initiate, receive, or participate in. In this way, they discover the patterns of kindness they engage in and see how kind acts enrich their lives. Teachers and students also begin to understand the concepts included in the Kindness Pledge. Through these basic practices, kindness becomes a way of life for the classroom community.

Sequence 2: Who We Are

For the classroom community to function well, it is important that individuals come to appreciate their diversity and at the same time find the common ground they share. This sequence of lessons is designed to help students honor their individual differences and discover their similarities. It is built on the premise that all of us belong to a number of cultures, each having distinguishing characteristics. Specifically, each of us comes from a culture made up of a unique conglomeration of heritage, family practices, and day-to-day experiences with others. When students honor differences and discover similarities, they lower the tension among themselves and find connections in a myriad of surprising ways.

Sequence 3: Circle of Kindness Meetings

In weekly Circle of Kindness meetings, students can express their feelings, clear up conflicts that arise among them, ask for forgiveness when needed, and look at different aspects of kindness and peacemaking within the school community.

In this sequence, students form a circle of 8 to 12 members, with an adult leader for each group. Adult leaders may include teachers and school support staff (counselors, social workers, aides, and so forth).

A specific agenda is observed in these circles. The repetition of this agenda allows students to feel safe and to speak freely. The steps are as follows:

1. Opening ritual

2. Checking in with feelings

3. Clearing a conflict, asking for forgiveness

4. Kindness Pledge activity

5. Closing ritual

The first four lessons in this sequence teach the agenda for the Circle of Kindness meeting: the opening ritual, checking in with feelings, clearing a conflict and asking for forgiveness, and the closing ritual. After students have participated in these lessons and know the meeting format, lessons begin to include the Kindness Pledge and other activities. Students in kindergarten through grade 3 experience Kindness Pledge activities drawn from the lessons in Sequence 4. Students in grades 4 through 8 participate in Kindness Pledge activities drawn from Sequence 4 and Sequence 5 (kindness dilemmas).

When students have completed the activities in these sequences, teachers may draw from other sources to continue weekly meetings relating to the tenets of the Kindness Pledge. Some good sources for activities include the following:

Building Assets Together: 135 Group Activities for Helping Youth Succeed, by Jolene L. Roehlkepartain. Minneapolis: Search Institute (1995).

How to Create Positive Relationships with Students: A Handbook of Group Activities and Teaching Strategies, by Michelle Karns. Champaign, IL: Research Press (1994).

Life Lessons for Young Adolescents: An Advisory Guide for Teachers, by Fred Schrumpf, Sharon Freiburg, and David Skadden. Champaign, IL: Research Press (1993).

Raising Student Aspirations: Classroom Activities (Grades K–5 and *Grades 6–8),* by Russell J. Quaglia and Christine M. Fox. Champaign, IL: Research Press (2003).

Reviving the Wonder: 76 Activities That Touch the Inner Spirit of Youth, by Ric Stuecker with Suze Rutherford. Champaign, IL: Research Press (2001).

Sequence 4: Living the Kindness Pledge

The lessons in this sequence give students the opportunity to examine each of the tenets of the Kindness Pledge in greater detail. Students and teachers focus on an activity relating to a different tenet each week. The lessons in this sequence help to put the Kindness Pledge and other schoolwide program activities into context.

As noted previously, you may use these lessons as the kindness activity portion of Circle of Kindness meetings, involving groups of 8 to 12 students. You may also choose to conduct the lessons in class groups of approximately 25 students.

Sequence 5: Kindness Dilemmas

The five dilemma stories in this sequence allow students to think through an everyday situation that involves a choice like the ones they face or see others face. Students must read the dilemma stories and determine what the kind or mature thing to do is in the situation. Each story is followed by a series of questions that deepen students' thinking and ask them to consider a different point of view. A closing lesson challenges students to create their own dilemma stories and questions, thus enriching this technique and encouraging further development of mature decision making. As noted previously, dilemma stories are excellent activities to use in Circle of Kindness meetings for grades 4 through 8.

Kind Classrooms
Lessons for Grades K–3

SEQUENCE I

Basic Practices for Building a Community

What Is Kindness? Using a Kindness Log

Purpose
▷ To help students learn the meaning of kindness and observe the kind acts they or others perform

Materials
▷ Chalkboard or easel pad
▷ Drawing and writing paper
▷ Colored markers
▷ Three-hole punch and binder (for Kindness Log)

Preparation
▷ None

Directions
1. Ask the students for examples of kindness they have experienced in the past week. On the chalkboard or easel pad, list each student's name and one act of kindness each has experienced.

2. Ask the group the following questions:
   ▷ Why would it be a good thing to treat one another with kindness?
   ▷ How would our classroom change if we always treated one another kindly and did kind things for one another? What would we feel?
   ▷ What obstacles to being kind have you noticed?
   ▷ How have you overcome these obstacles?

3. Hand out the paper and markers. Ask each student to draw a picture and write a story about the kind act they described.

4. Ask students to share their pictures and stories.

5. Explain that you will ask students to contribute a picture and story once a week for the next 4 weeks. You will collect these pictures and stories and save them in the Kindness Log (the three-ring binder).

6. Each week, review the kind acts that students contribute, and have volunteers present their pictures and stories to the class. Add these to the Kindness Log.

Discussion
▷ Were you surprised by the number of kind acts our class has experienced?
▷ How have you benefited from being kind?
▷ Did you notice any patterns of kindness? Specific times? Specific people? Specific ways of being kind?
▷ What do you think of keeping a Kindness Log?

Three Basic Rules

Purpose   ▷ To introduce the Three Basic Rules, which will be used in the classroom and throughout the school

Materials   ▷ Poster of the Three Basic Rules (see Appendix C)

                ▷ Chalkboard or easel pad

Preparation ▷ If you wish, make a larger display of the Three Basic Rules.

Directions   1. Explain that both in your classroom and in the entire school, students and teachers will be living according to the Three Basic Rules.

                2. Direct students' attention to the poster. Focus on each of the three rules in turn.

                3. As you discuss the first two questions for each rule, add the information the class volunteers to a chart on the chalkboard or easel pad like the example on page 68.

Rule 1: Be kind to yourself

How can you be kind to yourself?

How can you be unkind to yourself?

Why is it important to be kind to yourself?

What will we see, hear, and notice if you are being kind to yourself?

How can you be a better learner by being kind to yourself?

What specific things do good learners do to be kind to themselves?

Are you willing to take this challenge?

Rule 2: Be kind to one another

How can we be kind to one another in this classroom? In the school? In our neighborhoods and community?

How can we be unkind to one another in this classroom? In the school? In our neighborhoods and community?

Why is it important to be kind to one another?

What will we see if we are kind to one another? Hear? Notice?

How might kindness make you and your classmates better learners?

What are the best ways of working together?

Are you willing to take this challenge?

Rule 3: Be kind to this space

What is included in the words *this space?* (classroom, school, neighborhood, community)

How can we take care of and be kind to this space?

How can we be unkind to this space?

Why is it important to be kind to our space?

When we are kind to our space, what will we see? Hear? Notice?

How will kindness make this classroom a better place?

Are you willing to take this challenge?

Discussion

▷ Would you prefer to live in a classroom community that follows these simple rules or one that does not? Why?

▷ If someone were to follow these rules all his or her life, would that person be successful? Why or why not?

▷ How are the Three Basic Rules good "life rules"?

Sample Three Basic Rules Chart

Kind to yourself

1. *I come prepared to learn.*
2. *I listen to others.*
3. *I ask for forgiveness.*

Kind to one another

1. *I play with everyone.*
2. *I give others compliments.*
3. *I have a lot of friends.*

Kind to this space

1. *I put my materials away.*
2. *I can find things easily.*
3. *The classroom stays clean.*

Not kind to yourself

1. *I can't find my materials.*
2. *I talk when others talk.*
3. *I carry a grudge.*

Not kind to one another

1. *I only play with certain friends.*
2. *I make fun of others.*
3. *I have a lot of fights.*

Not kind to this space

1. *There is a mess in my desk.*
2. *My stuff always gets lost.*
3. *We have to clean a long time.*

Learning the Kindness Pledge

Purpose   ▷ To ensure that students understand all the tenets of the Kindness Pledge and can relate the pledge to their everyday lives

Materials   ▷ Poster of the Kindness Pledge (see Appendix C)

▷ Drawing paper

▷ Colored markers

Preparation ▷ If you wish, make a larger display of the Kindness Pledge.

Directions 1. Explain that both in your classroom and in the entire school, students and teachers will be living according to the Kindness Pledge.

2. Direct students' attention to the poster of the Kindness Pledge, then read the entire pledge aloud. Tell students that each numbered item is called a *tenet*. Ask students whether there are any other words they do not understand. If so, clarify.

3. Read or ask a volunteer to read each tenet. After each tenet, ask the following questions:

   ▷ Who can put this tenet in his or her own words to explain what it means?

   ▷ Does everyone understand what this tenet means?

   ▷ Who can give me an example from home or school that tells me about this part of the pledge?

   ▷ Is this tenet important? What would happen if we lived this way in our classroom and school?

4. Distribute markers and drawing paper. Ask students to choose one of the tenets to illustrate. You might suggest some situations—for example, two people talking about a problem, someone helping another learn a game, or someone being helpful in some other way.

5. When students have finished their drawings, post them on a wall or bulletin board.

6. Ask each student to stand beside his or her drawing and explain how it applies to the tenet of the Kindness Pledge.

Discussion ▷ Do you think you can live the Kindness Pledge here in our classroom and school?

▷ Where and when would you want to remember the Kindness Pledge?

▷ Which one of the tenets might you want to focus on first?

▷ Would it be a good idea if all of us focused on one tenet? Which one should we choose?

Doing My Best

Purpose   ▷ To introduce the concept of integrity: doing what you say you will do, doing your best, and living by a set of positive standards

Materials   ▷ Chalkboard or easel pad

▷ A large piece of poster board or a bulletin board

▷ Construction paper

▷ A craft stick for each student, one end red and the other end green

Preparation   ▷ With the construction paper, make a "pocket" for each student. Write students' names on the pockets, then attach them to the poster board or bulletin board.

▷ Color or paint the craft sticks so one end is red and the other green.

Directions   1. Ask students to suggest people in their lives whom they admire and wish they were like.

2. Ask students to suggest the qualities and characteristics they admire in these people. (Possible responses include trustworthiness, honesty, caring, and so forth.) List these characteristics on the chalkboard or easel pad.

3. Ask students whether the people they admire break their promises, lie, or cheat, then ask whether students would admire these people if they could not trust them or if these people let them down or failed to keep their promises.

4. Suggest that the word *integrity* means that you can be trusted to do your best, even when an adult isn't around, and that you live according to a set of positive principles and values, like the people they admire.

5. Divide the chalkboard or easel pad into two columns. On one side, write the words "Doing My Best." On the other, write "Just Getting By."

6. Ask the students for suggestions about how they either do their best or just get by in the following areas: as a student, as a family member, and as a member of the class. Record their ideas in the appropriate columns.

7. Show students the craft sticks and pockets. Tell them that at certain times during the day you will ask them to check the color of their sticks and decide at that time whether they are doing their best or just getting by. Explain that if they feel they have been doing their best, the green end of the stick

should be showing. If not, the red end should be showing, and they need to improve their behavior.

8. Several times throughout the day, ask students to check their sticks and move them if necessary to show whether or not they are doing their best.

9. At the end of the day, ask the students to give themselves a round of applause to congratulate themselves for working hard to do their best.

Discussion

▷ What makes it difficult for us to do our best all the time?

▷ Why do we sometimes choose just to get by?

▷ What happens when we don't live by our standards?

▷ What examples could you give to illustrate the idea of integrity?

▷ Is it possible to live up to your standards all the time? Why or why not?

Mail Pouches

Purpose ▷ To create a way students can honor one another and recognize the kind acts they receive

Materials ▷ One large manila envelope per student
▷ Colored markers
▷ Masking tape

Preparation ▷ Using a manila envelope and following the instructions to students, make a sample mail pouch for yourself, then post it on a wall or bulletin board.

Directions 1. Show your sample mail pouch to the class, and explain that students will be making a mail pouch like yours.

2. Distribute the manila envelopes and markers, then give students the following instructions:

   ▷ Decorate your mail pouch with pictures that show what things you like to do.

   ▷ Decorate the side of the envelope with the clasp so you can hang the mail pouch up by the flap.

   ▷ Make sure to put your name on your pouch.

3. Suggest to the class that whenever they wish, they can send their classmates kind notes or pictures (or even give their classmates Kindness Coupons they themselves have received for being kind—see Activity 14, page 43).

4. Post the mail pouches on an empty wall or bulletin board.

5. At least once a week, have students write notes or draw pictures to put in one another's mail pouches. Make sure each student gets mail each week.

Discussion ▷ When you get mail, how does that feel?
▷ Who are some of the people in your life you send mail to?
▷ On what occasions do we like to get mail?
▷ Have you ever gotten mail when you felt down or sad?
▷ What could you do when someone you know feels sad?

SEQUENCE 2

Who We Are

LESSONS

Trains

Purpose
▷ To let students see that, even though they are each unique and different, they are also a part of the classroom community

Materials
▷ A wooden train whistle (or another type of whistle if a wooden one is unavailable)

▷ *Optional:* One train engineer's hat per group of five to eight students

Preparation
▷ Enlist the aid of another adult or older student for each group of five to eight students.

▷ Locate a large room without furniture in which to conduct the activity.

Directions
1. Arrange the class in random groups, with an adult or older student leader for each group.

2. Tell students that they are train cars, and you are going to line them up in different ways to form new trains.

3. Give the groups a directive from the following choices:
   ▷ Tallest to shortest
   ▷ Youngest to oldest
   ▷ Smallest feet to largest feet
   ▷ Alphabetical order
   ▷ Numerical order, using the number of their house address
   ▷ Color of hair: blonds, brunettes, redheads
   ▷ Color of eyes: brown, green, blue, hazel

4. Each time students line up, put an engineer's hat on the first child. That child becomes the engineer.

5. Ask the children lined up behind the engineer to put their hands on the shoulders of the child in front.

6. Tell students that when you blow the whistle, the train may leave the station and take a trip in a large circle (if you are outside) or around the room (if you are inside). Tell students that when you blow the whistle again, they must stop.

7. At each stop, give the "trains" a new directive. Repeat until all the children have had a chance to be the engineer.

Discussion

▷ Look around the group. In what ways are we each unique and different? In what ways are we alike?

▷ Did you like being the engineer? The train? What made each role fun?

▷ Can you have a train if everyone wants to be an engineer at the same time?

▷ What did you have to do to become a train?

Power Circle

Purpose   ▷ To encourage students to examine their values, beliefs, and actions, and to observe those of others

Materials   ▷ None

Preparation ▷ Add any of your own ideas to the list provided in the lesson.

▷ Locate a large room with no furniture in which to conduct the activity.

Directions   ### Part I

1. Ask students to form a large circle, facing one another.

2. Ask one of the students to walk across the circle. Suggest to the group that this student has demonstrated one way of crossing the circle. Ask another student to cross in a different way. Ask every student to cross the circle using a different movement—hopping, skipping—ways they invent.

3. When all have crossed, ask students to form groups of three with the people closest to them.

4. Ask each group to cross the circle together in a unique way, different from that of the other groups.

Part 2

1. When all the groups have crossed, ask students to cross the circle individually when they agree with or have had an experience you announce. (Students should cross with no special movements and without discussion or comment.)

2. Give instructions like the following, one at a time.

Cross the circle if you ever . . .

enjoyed eating ice cream.

worried about flunking a test.

built a tree house.

lied to your parents.

cheated on a test.

took the blame for someone else.

were made fun of because of how you look.

worried that your parents might get a divorce.

lived with only one parent.

cleaned your room without being asked.

worried you would not be picked for a team.

spread rumors or gossip.

waited for a call that didn't come.

thought other people were more popular than you.

made fun of someone else.

worried about how you look.

thought your family was poor.

let someone convince you to do something you wish you hadn't.

apologized when you were wrong.

Discussion

▷ Was it ever difficult to cross the circle?

▷ Did you ever not cross even when you could have?

▷ How did it feel to cross the circle? By yourself? With other people?

▷ Were you surprised by who crossed the circle? Do you see any of your classmates differently now?

▷ Some of the suggestions were actions that break rules or challenge someone's personal integrity. Is it okay to do these things because lots of others do? Why or why not?

Card Villages

Purpose   ▷ To create a metaphor for the classroom as a community

Materials   ▷ 300 to 500 index cards for every group of three to five students

Preparation ▷ Locate a large room with no furniture in which to conduct the activity.

Directions

1. Randomly form groups of three to five students each.

2. Give each group a set of index cards. Tell them they will be building a card town or village.

3. Tell them they can only bend the cards one way: so the shorter ends of the card are together. Fold a card to show them.

4. Tell them that each group will build houses, buildings, roads, and bridges. Let them know that the roads and bridges must connect to at least three other groups' villages.

5. Answer any questions, then let students build. When a group has used all the cards, the group is finished.

6. When all the groups have finished, ask students to form a large circle around their villages and sit down.

Discussion   ▷ How do you like the village you made?

▷ Was it hard to build a village?

▷ Could you have built the village by yourself? How long do you think that would have taken?

▷ Is building with your classmates more fun than working alone?

▷ How is our classroom like a village?

Class Quilt

Purpose   ▷ To create a visual metaphor for the classroom community

Materials   ▷ A real quilt

▷ Camera and film, digital camera, or Polaroid camera

▷ Old magazines

▷ Colored paper

▷ Scissors

▷ Glue

Preparation   ▷ Take each student's picture with the camera, and have the film developed. (If you have a digital or Polaroid camera, you can proceed directly to the rest of the activity.)

▷ Cut the colored paper along the bottom to form an 8-by-8-inch square.

▷ Create a sample quilt square, including your own photograph and information.

Directions   1. Show the class the quilt you have brought. Discuss how the large quilt is made up of smaller pieces, each one important to the whole design.

2. Show the class your quilt square, and explain its content.

3. Tell students that they will be making their own quilt squares. Let them know that each of them is important to the class and that all the squares they make are important to the final quilt that they will make as a class.

4. Distribute the scissors, glue, paper, and magazines.

5. Ask the students to select three to five magazine pictures that represent who they are and what they like to do. Have them cut these out and glue their photographs and magazine pictures on the colored paper.

6. Connect all the quilt squares to form the class quilt, then hang it on a wall in your classroom.

Discussion   ▷ What do you like about the quilt squares you made?

▷ What did we have to do to make the quilt?

▷ What would happen if any one student's square was not a part of the quilt?

▷ Is everyone in our class important?

▷ If we are all important, how should we treat one another?

Note Some teachers make actual quilts by having the photos transferred to cloth squares. Students sew other symbols and decorations on their squares, then sew the blocks together.

Class Flag

Purpose	▷ To create a symbol for the classroom community
Materials	▷ Several different flags or pictures of flags
	▷ A piece of nylon (the type used for flags and kites) approximately 3 by 5 feet in size
	▷ A variety of colored nylon swatches (on which every child will trace the outline of his or her hand)
	▷ Flagpole (a broomstick or heavy dowel rod will work)
	▷ Fabric glue, markers, and scissors
Preparation	▷ Select a way to attach the flag to the flagpole (a sleeve or grommets).

Directions

1. Show the class a variety of flags or pictures of flags. Discuss the idea that a flag is a symbol, a real thing that stands for something we believe in, and that when we honor a flag we are honoring a belief.

2. Explain that the class is going to make a class flag. Tell them that the symbol on their flag will be their handprint. (If a different symbol is more meaningful to students, they could create the flag accordingly.)

3. Help each child trace his or her handprint on a piece of nylon and then cut it out.

4. Print or have each student print his or her name on the hand.

5. Glue each handprint onto the flag.

6. Attach the flag to the pole, then hang the flag in a prominent place.

7. If you wish, each morning after the pledge of allegiance to the flag of the United States, have students face the class flag and say the Kindness Pledge.

Discussion

▷ What do you like about our flag?

▷ Why do we honor flags?

▷ Why do we have a Kindness Pledge?

▷ Why is it important to honor the Kindness Pledge?

SEQUENCE 3

Circle of Kindness Meetings

LESSONS

Creating an Opening Ritual

Purpose ▷ To introduce the idea of the Circle of Kindness meeting and have small groups create a ritual to define its opening

Materials ▷ Poster of the Circle of Kindness Meeting Agenda (see Appendix C)

Preparation ▷ If you wish, make a larger display of the Circle of Kindness Meeting Agenda.

▷ Enlist the aid of an adult leader for each group of 8 to 12 students.

Note: If possible, assign adult leaders to the same small groups during all Circle of Kindness meetings.

Directions 1. Explain to the class that as part of the Kindness Initiative the class will be having something called Circle of Kindness meetings. You might say, for example:

> A Circle of Kindness meeting is a special time, different from the rest of our school day. Each week, we will get together in small groups to find out how we are feeling; clear up any conflicts and ask for forgiveness, if we need to; and look at different aspects of kindness and peacemaking in our classroom.

2. Show students the poster of the Circle of Kindness Meeting Agenda, and explain that, to begin, these meetings need a special ritual.

3. Ask students to give examples of any opening rituals they know about. For example:

   ▷ Playing the national anthem before a ball game

   ▷ A team's putting their hands one on top of the other in a circle before a game

   ▷ Boy Scouts and Girl Scouts reciting the scouting oath before a meeting

4. Divide the class into groups of 8 to 12 students, each with an adult leader. Let groups know they will be developing an opening ritual for their group.

5. Have group leaders help students generate ideas. At this level, leaders will need to do most of this. It is important, however, to include students' input. For example:

   An opening song: Have the group select a theme from a favorite television show or a familiar children's song, then solicit words and phrases from the Kindness Pledge that they might include. Help them combine the words and melody.

An opening cheer: Solicit words and phrases students might want to include. Lead the group in creating a rhythm with claps, finger snaps, and thigh slaps, then set words and phrases to that rhythm.

6. Give each group of students a chance to practice their ritual, then have each group perform their ritual for the other groups.

Discussion
▷ Did you like making a ritual for your group?

▷ Will you agree to use this ritual to begin each Circle of Kindness meeting?

▷ What was good about ideas for the ritual that didn't get included?

Note
The class could also create a simple rap or verse that expresses the Circle of Kindness themes.

Checking In with Feelings

Purpose ▷ To give students a way to tell their classmates how they are feeling

Materials ▷ Poster of the Circle of Kindness Meeting Agenda (from Lesson 3.1)

▷ Plain paper plates

▷ Markers

▷ Craft sticks

▷ Glue

Preparation ▷ Glue the paper plates to the craft sticks to prepare five masks per student. On each mask, draw a face representing a different feeling word: *mad, sad, glad, scared,* and *guilty.* (Drawings can be very simple.)

▷ Enlist the aid of your group leaders.

Directions 1. Have the class form their small groups, then with their group leader's assistance perform their opening ritual.

2. Refer students to the poster of the Circle of Kindness Meeting Agenda, and explain that in this lesson they will learn how to "check in" with their feelings and ask for forgiveness, if they need to.

3. Tell students that most feelings can be expressed by the words *mad, sad, glad, scared,* and *guilty.* For example:

▷ I'm feeling *mad* because a friend of mine didn't send me an invitation to his party.

▷ I'm feeling *sad* because I'm going to miss the field trip.

▷ I'm feeling *glad* because the rain finally stopped.

▷ I'm feeling a little *scared* because I have a test this afternoon.

▷ I'm feeling *guilty* because I told my mom I'd clean my room, and then I played on the computer instead.

4. Give each student five masks, one for each feeling. In their groups, ask students to hold up the mask that most expresses their feelings right now.

5. After all of the students have checked in with a feeling mask, ask each one to explain briefly to the group how the mask represents his or her feelings.

Discussion
- ▷ Is it easy to talk about how we feel? If it is difficult, why?
- ▷ What might happen if other people know how we feel?
- ▷ Did it surprise you that other people felt the same as you?
- ▷ Were you surprised at how someone else in your group felt?
- ▷ When other people talk about their feelings, does it make it easier for you to do so?
- ▷ Do you feel closer to other people if you know how they feel?

Note

If you wish, let students make and draw their own masks. Older students could also assist in creating the masks.

As a variation, you could use colors instead of masks to designate the feelings (yellow is glad, red is mad, blue is sad, orange is scared, green is guilty). Have each child "check in" with a color by holding up a colored chip or slip of paper, or simply by saying the color.

Clearing a Conflict, Asking for Forgiveness

Purpose   ▷ To teach students a four-point process that they can use to resolve conflicts and ask for forgiveness

Materials   ▷ Poster of the Circle of Kindness Meeting Agenda (from Lesson 3.1)

▷ Feelings masks (from Lesson 3.2)

▷ Four-Point Process for Clearing a Conflict and Asking for Forgiveness (see Appendix C)

Preparation ▷ If you wish, make a larger display of the four-point process.

▷ Enlist the aid of your group leaders.

▷ Prepare two role plays between yourself and one of your leaders—one to demonstrate how the four points are applied to clear a conflict and the other to ask for forgiveness. (For examples, see the role plays on page 93.)

Directions   1. Have the class form their small groups, perform their opening ritual, and check in with their feelings masks.

2. Refer to the third step on the Circle of Kindness Meeting Agenda: clearing a conflict, asking for forgiveness. Suggest that anyone who is feeling angry or in conflict with another person or who needs to be forgiven by another person will have a hard time paying attention to what is going on in the classroom.

3. Direct students' attention to the poster of the four-point process. Explain that in this lesson students will learn how to use the four-point process to help them clear up conflicts and ask for forgiveness.

4. With your adult partner, conduct your role plays of clearing a conflict and asking for forgiveness. Refer to the points on the poster as you do.

5. Have group leaders ask students to look around their group to see whether there is anyone with whom they are in conflict or from whom they need to ask forgiveness. (If no one volunteers, go on to the discussion questions.)

6. If the situation is about clearing a conflict, the group leader asks the two students to stand and face each other. The leader stands to the side to provide coaching if necessary.

7. The leader prompts the student who needs to clear a conflict as follows:

Point 1: State the *data. (What happened?)*

Point 2: State your *feeling. (Encourage students to use the words* mad, sad, glad, scared, *and* guilty.)

Point 3: State your *judgment. (Why do you think the situation happened?)*

Point 4: State your *choice. (What do you want from the other person?)*

8. If the situation is one of asking for forgiveness, the leader brings the two students to the middle of the circle, then goes through the same process.

Discussion

▷ Is the four-point process you learned a good way to resolve conflicts and ask forgiveness?

▷ What usually happens between two people who are angry with each other or feel misused?

▷ Is it scary to do deal with a conflict or ask forgiveness in this way? If so, why?

▷ How could you use this process outside of our Circle of Kindness meetings?

▷ Would it help to have a teacher or another adult guide you?

Note

When doing the role plays, point out that conflicts may not always be resolved in a positive way and that people don't always accept apologies. The process is still worth trying, even though it might not have a positive outcome.

Sample Role Plays

Clearing a Conflict

Teacher: Mary, what happened on the playground?

Mary: *(Data)* Hilda said she would play with me, but then I saw her playing with Ramona.

Teacher: How did that make you feel?

Mary: *(Feeling)* Bad. I wanted to play with Hilda, and Ramona didn't want me to play with them.

Teacher: Did you feel sad? Mad? Both?

Mary: Mostly sad, but a little mad, too.

Teacher: Why do you think this happened?

Mary: *(Judgment)* Hilda doesn't like me any more?

Teacher: What do you want?

Mary: *(Choice)* I want to play with Hilda. I want her to like me.

Teacher: *(To Hilda)* Do you want to say anything to Mary?

Hilda: I like you, Mary. You were late coming out, and I got playing with the others, and I forgot I promised. Don't be mad at me.

Mary: Will you play with me tomorrow?

Hilda: Sure.

Asking for Forgiveness

Teacher: Sebastian, Jorge has something he wants to say to you.

Jorge: Sebastian, can I talk to you?

Sebastian: Sure.

Teacher: What do you need to say, Jorge?

Jorge: *(Data)* Yesterday I promised to play games with you on your computer at your house. When I got home, Manuel came over. I was surprised. I forgot to come over or to call you.

Teacher: *(To Jorge)* How did that make you feel?

Jorge: *(Feeling)* I had fun with Manuel, but this morning when I saw Sebastian I remembered and I felt sad. *(Judgment)* I should have remembered. I'm sorry I forgot.

Teacher: What do you want to happen?

Jorge: *(Choice)* I don't want Sebastian to be mad at me, and maybe we could play this afternoon.

Sebastian: That would be cool. Thanks, Jorge.

Creating a Closing Ritual

Purpose   ▷   To help students create a closing ritual to indicate that the Circle of Kindness meeting has ended

Materials   ▷   Poster of the Circle of Kindness Meeting Agenda (from Lesson 3.1)

▷   Feelings masks (from Lesson 3.2)

▷   Poster of the Kindness Pledge (from Lesson 1.3)

Preparation ▷   Enlist the aid of your group leaders.

Directions   1. Have students get into their small groups, conduct their opening ritual, and check in with feelings. If necessary, students may use the four-point process to clear conflicts or ask for forgiveness.

2. Suggest that, like the opening ritual, the Circle of Kindness meeting needs a closing ritual. Refer students to the poster of the Circle of Kindness Meeting Agenda, and say something like this:

By having our opening ritual, we know we are in our special Circle of Kindness time. We find out how we are feeling and clear up any conflicts among us. If we need to, we ask for forgiveness. Then we are ready for a kindness activity. Before we do a kindness activity, though, we need to know when our circle time is over and we go back to class. To do this, we need to create a closing ritual. This ritual will tell us that our meeting is finished.

3. Have leaders help their groups generate ideas. As is true for the opening ritual, in K–3 groups, leaders most likely will have to direct the process. However, it is important to ask students for their ideas. For example:

▷   One group holds hands and shouts, "It's cool to be kind," then everyone lets go at the same time: "1, 2, 3 . . . Break!"

▷   Another group stands holding hands, and each person is given the opportunity to say in one sentence what he or she liked about the meeting.

▷   Another group slaps thighs, claps hands, and snaps fingers, then all cheer, "Kindness rocks!"

4. Have each group perform their ritual for the other students in the class.

5. Let students know that they will perform their closing rituals at the end of future Circle of Kindness meetings.

Discussion

▷ Why do our groups need closing rituals?

▷ How is your group's closing ritual meaningful to you?

▷ What did you like about other groups' rituals?

▷ Will you agree to use your rituals at the end of each Circle of Kindness meeting?

Kindness Pledge Activity

Purpose	▷ To strengthen the use of the Circle of Kindness meeting and enhance students' understanding of the first tenet of the Kindness Pledge: seeking the positive
Materials	▷ Poster of the Circle of Kindness Meeting Agenda (from Lesson 3.1)
	▷ Feelings masks (from Lesson 3.2)
	▷ Poster of the Kindness Pledge (from Lesson 1.3)
	▷ Materials listed for Lesson 4.1 (see page 99)
Preparation	▷ Enlist the aid of your group leaders.

Directions

1. Have students get into their small groups, conduct their opening ritual, check in with feelings, and—if necessary—use the four-point process to clear conflicts or ask for forgiveness.

2. Refer students to the poster of the Kindness Pledge, and let them know that in this lesson they will be doing an activity to learn about the first tenet of the pledge: seeking the positive.

3. Conduct Lesson 4.1.

4. Explain that from now on, the Circle of Kindness will include an activity that relates to the Kindness Pledge.

5. Ask the discussion questions, then have the groups perform their closing rituals.

Discussion

▷ How do you feel about using our Circle of Kindness meetings to learn more about the Kindness Pledge?

▷ Why is it important for us to do activities that relate to the Kindness Pledge?

▷ What part of the meetings do you like best? Least?

▷ Is there anything you wish we could add to our meetings?

SEQUENCE 4

Living the Kindness Pledge

LESSONS

Seeking the Positive

Purpose   ▷ To give students a chance to see what is positive about their classmates and to communicate that understanding through praise

Materials   ▷ One large sheet of plain newsprint or easel-pad paper per student (approximately 3 by 5 feet)

▷ Colored markers

▷ Old magazines

▷ Scissors

▷ Glue

▷ Masking tape

Preparation   ▷ None

Directions   1. Explain that students will be making "praise posters." The praise poster is a way to express their own positive qualities and to recognize the positive qualities of their classmates.

2. Give students the paper and markers. Let them know that their posters should include their names and be decorated with designs like those on a picture frame. They should leave at least two thirds of the poster blank.

3. Discuss the importance of making sure everyone is included: Tell students to make sure to write, draw, or glue a picture on every other student's poster during the week. (Teachers and other adults working with the students should model this by adding their own words, drawings, and pictures.)

4. Hang the posters around the classroom at a level where it is easy for other students to write compliments, make drawings, or glue on pictures. Sample ideas are as follows:

   ▷ "I had fun playing foursquare with you today."

   ▷ "I think you're cool."

   ▷ A drawing of two students eating lunch together.

   ▷ A magazine picture of an athlete (to show you think the student is a good athlete).

   ▷ A picture of something you know the student really likes.

   Students can sign their names next to the words and pictures they put on the posters.

5. Have students add words of praise, compliments, and drawings to one another's posters each day at a special time. Make sure students are giving praise and compliments to all their fellow students.

6. At the end of the week, when the posters are full, let students take them home.

Discussion
  ▷ Who in our lives gives us the most praise?
  ▷ How often do we praise others?
  ▷ How do we choose to praise others?
  ▷ How does it feel to give praise? To receive praise?

Putting Down Put-Downs

Purpose   ▷ To teach students a variety of ways of dealing with put-downs

Materials   ▷ Chalkboard or easel pad

▷ Purchased puppets or simple stick puppets of boys' and girls' faces (which you or your students can make)

Preparation   ▷ Arrange chairs in a semicircle, leaving enough space open to conduct role plays.

Directions   1. Ask the class to describe all the ways students put one another down. List these briefly on the chalkboard or easel pad. Responses might include the following:

▷ Roll their eyes when you say something.

▷ Make fun of you.

▷ Not let you play with them.

▷ Call you a name.

2. Select two students to use two of the puppets to portray a situation where one puts the other down. Suggest that the reaction of the puppet being put down will likely be hurt, anger, or both.

3. Have the students perform the puppet role play.

4. Ask for suggestions from the class as to how a person in this situation being put down could react in a positive way, and list responses on the chalkboard or easel pad. For example:

▷ Count from 1 to 10 before reacting.

▷ Breathe deeply.

▷ Say how you feel, using an "I" statement (for example, "When you make fun of my clothes, I feel angry and hurt, and I want you to stop doing that").

▷ Do not respond—just walk away.

5. Pair up the rest of the students. Ask each pair to prepare a short puppet role play that demonstrates a different put-down situation.

6. Perform the role plays, one at a time. After each role play, ask these questions:

▷ Was the role play realistic?

▷ What techniques did the role player use to respond?

▷ Were these techniques effective?

▷ Could you use these techniques in your daily life?

Discussion ▷ Why do some people put other people down?

▷ What is the effect of put-downs on our class community?

▷ What would happen if we didn't use put-downs?

▷ Will you commit to putting down put-downs?

Honoring Our Differences, Discovering Our Similarities

Purpose   ▷ To allow students to honor individual differences among their classmates and discover characteristics they have in common

Materials   ▷ Chalkboard or easel pad

Preparation   ▷ Locate a large room with no furniture in which to conduct the activity.

Directions   1. Start with everyone in a large circle in the center of the room.

2. Say to the group:

   I am going to ask you to step into the center of the circle according to the description or category I give. Each time I give you a category, all the people who have that description should step into the circle. For example, I might ask you to group yourselves by the color of your hair.

3. Have students who have the same color hair (blond, red, brown, black) form separate groups.

4. Have students regroup according to the following criteria:

   All the people with the same size feet as you

   All the people who are 3 feet tall or taller

   All the people who like pepperoni pizza

   All the people born in another state

   All the people who have traveled to another state

   All the people who play baseball

   All the people who love to read

5. Add some more personal descriptions. For example:

   All the people from single-parent homes

   Anyone who has felt left out

   Anyone who has been put down in the past week

   Anyone who has put someone else down in the past week

   Anyone who has received a compliment in the past week

   Anyone who has felt listened to by someone else

   Anyone who needs forgiveness

   Anyone who needs to forgive

6. On the chalkboard or easel pad, list students' responses to the first two discussion questions.

Discussion

▷ What similarities did you notice?

▷ What differences did you notice?

▷ How did you feel when you learned that a lot of your classmates have things in common with you? When only a few do? When you are the only one who fits the description?

▷ Did you learn anything new about people you might have known for some time?

▷ Were you surprised about what you learned? In what way?

▷ Why are both similarities and differences important in a group of people?

Healing Our Hurts

Purpose   ▷ To challenge students to find ways to heal hurts among their classmates

Materials   ▷ Drawing paper and markers

▷ Craft sticks

▷ Masking tape

▷ Chalkboard or easel pad

▷ Poster of the Four-Point Process for Clearing a Conflict and Asking for Forgiveness (from Lesson 3.3)

Preparation ▷ Arrange chairs in a semicircle, allowing an open space where students can conduct role plays.

Directions   1. Distribute the paper, markers, craft sticks, and tape.

2. Ask each student to draw a large picture of a boy's or girl's face, depending on which sex they are. (These pictures will become masks, so they should be large enough to cover the students' faces.)

3. Have students cut their pictures out and tape them onto their sticks.

4. Ask students whether at times outside of class they have hurt someone else's feelings and wanted to apologize. Encourage them to describe specific incidents, and list these examples on the chalkboard or easel pad.

5. Get students' ideas on how they decided they had hurt someone. For example:

> You notice that your good friend doesn't come over to play with you on the playground. You realize he or she is mad because you had lunch with another friend and didn't invite him or her to join you.

6. Direct students' attention to the poster of the four-point process, and remind them of the way they learned to apologize in Circle of Kindness meetings:

Point 1: State the *data. (What happened?)*

Point 2: State your *feeling.*

Point 3: State your *judgment. (Why do you think the problem happened?)*

Point 4: State your *choice. (What do you want from the other person?)*

7. Suggest that students can use the four-point process to apologize at any time, not just when they are together in their Circles of Kindness. Let students know that when they apologize, it is a good idea to do it privately, away from other students.

8. Ask for a volunteer to help you role-play this apology:

   Data: The other day, I ate lunch with another friend and didn't ask you to join us.

   Feeling: I saw your face when you saw us, and I felt bad.

   Judgment: I was having fun, and I just didn't think about how it might hurt you until I saw you later.

   Choice: I want us to be friends. Maybe we could do something at my house this afternoon.

9. Have students pair up. Ask each pair to create a role play showing one person apologizing to the other by using the four-point process. Have them hold the masks to their faces as they do so.

10. Ask for volunteers to perform their role plays for the class. After each role play, ask these questions:

    ▷ Did the role play seem real?

    ▷ Do you think the person would accept this apology? Why or why not?

Discussion

▷ Would you forgive someone if the person apologized by using the four-point process?

▷ Has anyone apologized by doing something nice for you? If so, what? *(Responses may include writing you a note, giving you a present, or making you a card.)*

▷ Which ways of apologizing did you like? Which ones might you use if you hurt someone?

▷ What happens if we hurt others' feelings and don't apologize?

Note

In K–1 classes, you may want to invite older students (from grades 4–8) to create and perform simple role plays or have two adults perform typical situations.

Listening to One Other

Purpose ▷ To increase the ability of students to listen to other people

Materials ▷ Chalkboard or easel pad

Preparation ▷ Locate a large room with no furniture in which to conduct the activity.

Directions

1. Create pairs of students.

2. Ask one student to stand behind the other, placing his or her hands on the other student's shoulders. The student in front is the "car." The student in the back is the "driver."

3. Ask cars to put up their "bumpers" by placing their hands in front of them, then ask cars to close their eyes.

4. Ask drivers to give oral directions to their cars to drive their cars safely around the room without any crashes.

5. If any crashes occur, ask car and driver to sit down.

6. Reverse the roles of cars and drivers.

Discussion

▷ When you were the driver, did you feel that your car listened to you?

If yes: How did that feel?

If no: If your car didn't listen to you, what happened?

▷ How often at home do you and your family sit down and talk to one another?

▷ How do you know when someone is really listening to you?

▷ What do you think are some good ways to show someone else you are listening? *(List students' responses on the chalkboard or easel pad—for example, nodding your head, asking questions, repeating what the person said in your own words, adding your own ideas at appropriate times.)*

Honoring Heroes

Purpose   ▷ To encourage students to identify adults in their lives who support them and to make closer connections with these adults

Materials ▷ Hero Recognition Certificate
              ▷ Colored markers
              ▷ Glue
              ▷ *Optional:* Photographs of the individuals students select as personal heroes

Preparation ▷ Make three to five copies of the Hero Recognition Certificate for each student.
              ▷ Ask students to bring in three to five photographs of people they consider to be heroes in their lives. If students are not able to bring the photos, they may draw pictures of their heroes on the certificates instead.

Directions 1. Distribute the Hero Recognition Certificates, markers, and glue to students.
              2. Ask students to decorate the certificates and fill in the blanks.
              3. When they have finished, ask students to glue their photographs, if they have them, onto the certificates (one per certificate).
              4. Create a classroom "Hall of Heroes" by posting at least one certificate per student.
              5. Ask students to hand deliver certificates to each of the heroes they selected.

Discussion ▷ How did you decide who the heroes in your life are?
              ▷ What characteristics do your heroes have?
              ▷ How often do you talk with your heroes?
              ▷ What special things do you do together?
              ▷ What do you hope to learn from your heroes?

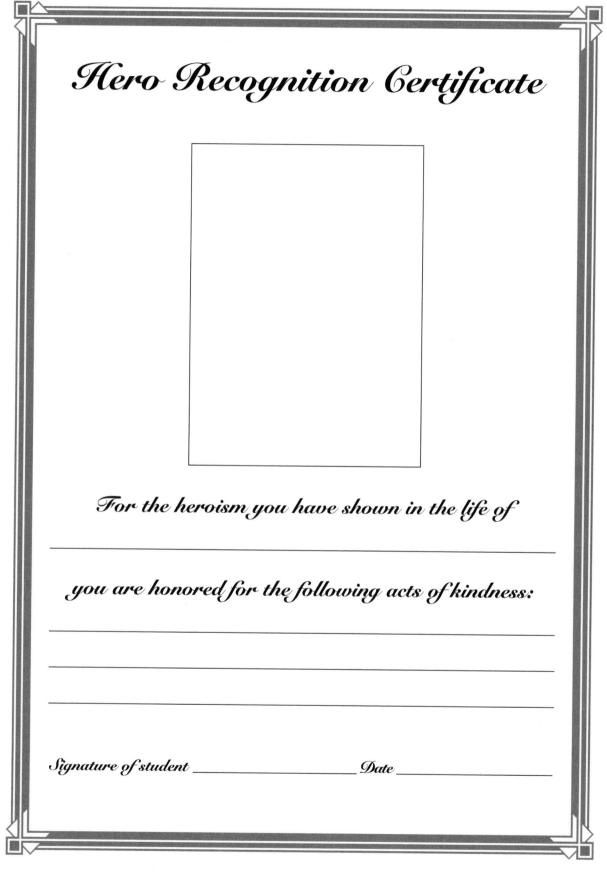

Hero Recognition Certificate

For the heroism you have shown in the life of

_____

you are honored for the following acts of kindness:

_____

_____

_____

Signature of student _____ *Date* _____

Reaching Higher for Success

Purpose
- To help students learn the importance of setting goals and developing specific steps to achieve their goals

Materials
- Goal Sheet
- Colored markers
- Gold stars or stickers

Preparation
- Every week, make one copy of the Goal Sheet for each student.

Directions
1. At the beginning of the week, negotiate with each student a specific goal he or she hopes to reach by the end of that week. Goals can be for achievement (for example, reading a simple book) or behavior (for example, staying seated during seatwork time).

2. Distribute the Goal Sheets, and help each student decide on a personal goal. Have the student write the goal on the sheet, then draw a picture on the sheet to illustrate the goal.

3. Post the completed sheets on the classroom wall or bulletin board.

4. Each time you see a child achieve a goal, give him or her a gold star or sticker to put on the Goal Sheet.

5. At the end of the week, give a simple reward to those who have achieved their goals and to those who have shown effort in working toward their goals. For those students still working on goals, meet and discuss how they can successfully reach their goals—or construct different goals.

Discussion
- Why is it good to have goals?
- What kinds of goals are hard for you to meet?
- Do you always need a reward to achieve a goal?
- How do you feel when you get a reward for reaching a goal?

Goal Sheet

Name _____ **Week of** _____

My goal _____

Living Our Dreams

Purpose   ▷ To help students establish positive dreams for themselves in the future

Materials   ▷ A book from the library with detailed instructions for making simple kites

▷ Materials specified for constructing and flying kites (nylon fabric or paper, glue, wooden framework, string, and so forth)

▷ Drawing paper

▷ Colored markers

Preparation   ▷ Select one or two simple kite designs.

▷ Find a safe, convenient place to fly kites.

Directions   *Activity 1: Class Kite*

1. Meet individually with each student to help him or her select one dream he or she has for the school year.

2. When you have spoken with all of the students, tell the class that, with their help and ideas, you are going to construct a class "Kindness Kite."

3. Hand out drawing paper and markers, and ask students to create drawings they would like to include on the kite. Explain that these drawings should illustrate the tenets of the Kindness Pledge in some way.

4. Hang up all the designs, then ask the students to select three to five they would like to put on the class kite. (One way of doing this is to give each student a small stick-on dot to put on the designs they like best.)

5. Make a mock-up of the kite, using the selected designs. Incorporate colors the students would like and make any changes they suggest.

6. Construct the kite according to the instructions. On the back of the kite, have each student write his or her dream. Discuss with students how we want to let our dreams soar.

7. On a good kite-flying day, take the kite to a safe area and fly it with the class.

Activity 2: Kite Festival

1. Challenge students to create a kite to fly in a kite festival. Tell them this is a home project, and give them several weeks to design and construct their kites.

2. Create, duplicate, and distribute requirements for a standard diamond-shaped kite. For example:

   ▷ Kites should be 3 to 5 feet in length, 2 to 4 feet in width.

   ▷ Kites may be made of nylon, wrapping paper, or mailing paper.

   ▷ Decorations should reflect concepts and tenets from the Kindness Pledge

3. Display the kites in a central area of your school. Keep the emphasis positive: Remember that this is a celebration, not a contest.

4. On a great kite-flying day, take the kites out and let them soar. Encourage students to share their kites with one another, especially students who did not make kites.

Discussion

▷ How did you like our kite activity?

▷ What is the difference between a celebration and a contest?

▷ Why do you think we like contests?

▷ Is it more fun when there are no winners or losers, or do you prefer to have a contest?

▷ Who were the winners at our kite celebration?

▷ What are some other times we like to celebrate?

▷ Whom do we invite to our celebrations?

Note

If you think students in your class may have difficulty making individual kites, you might want to invite older students or adult mentors to help students after school. The kite festival can also be a schoolwide event sponsored by the Kindness Initiative.

Kind Classrooms
Lessons for Grades 4–8

SEQUENCE 1

Basic Practices for Building a Community

LESSONS

What Is Kindness? Using a Kindness Log

Purpose
▷ To help students learn the meaning of kindness and observe the kind acts they or others perform

Materials
▷ Chalkboard or easel pad
▷ Kindness Log (10 per student)
▷ Folders (one per student)

Preparation
▷ Photocopy the Kindness Log. Put one set of copies per student in a folder.
▷ Prepare a sample Kindness Log for illustration.

Directions
1. Ask the group for examples of kindness they have experienced in the past week.
2. Have the group explain why it might be a good thing to treat one another with kindness. Make a list of reasons on the chalkboard or easel pad.
3. Ask the group these questions:
   ▷ How would the climate in the classroom change if students always treated one another kindly and performed kind acts?
   ▷ Do you see any obstacles to being kind to one another? If so, what are some ways you could overcome these obstacles?
4. Hand out the folders and Kindness Logs.
5. Explain how to fill out the Kindness Log by discussing the sample you made.
6. Tell the students that during the next 4 weeks they will need to record at least 10 kind acts they have performed or received. Let them know that there will be a review day at the end of the second and fourth weeks, when they will share their logs.
7. On the review day, have volunteers share their Kindness Logs with the group. Ask each volunteer the discussion questions.

Discussion
▷ Were you surprised by the number of kind acts you experienced?
▷ What obstacles to being kind did you notice?

▷ How did you overcome any obstacles you met?

▷ How did you benefit from being kind?

▷ Did you notice any patterns of kindness? Specific times? Specific people? Specific types of kind acts?

Kindness Log

Name _____ **Date** _____

Answer the following questions to describe one act of kindness you performed or received.

1. What time of day was it? _____

2. Where were you? _____

3. Whom were you with? _____

4. What happened? *(Describe in detail.)*

_____

_____

_____

_____

5. What was the result?

_____

_____

6. If you performed a kind act, on a scale of 1 to 7, how kind were you?

       Somewhat   1   2   3   4   5   6   7   Extremely

7. How did it feel, on a scale of 1 to 7, to perform or receive a kind act?

       Okay   1   2   3   4   5   6   7   Great

Three Basic Rules

Purpose ▷ To introduce the Three Basic Rules, which will be used in the classroom and throughout the school

Materials ▷ Poster of the Three Basic Rules (see Appendix C)

▷ Chalkboard or easel pad

Preparation ▷ If you wish, make a larger display of the Three Basic Rules.

Directions 1. Direct students' attention to the poster. Focus on each of the three rules on the poster in turn.

2. For each of the rules, ask the following questions. As you discuss each rule, add the information the class volunteers to a chart on the chalkboard or easel pad like the sample given on page 124.

Rule 1: Be kind to yourself

How can you be kind to yourself?

How can you be unkind to yourself?

Why is it important to be kind to yourself?

What will we see, hear, and notice if you are being kind to yourself?

How can you be a better learner by being kind to yourself?

What specific things do good learners do to be kind to themselves?

Are you willing to take this challenge?

Rule 2: Be kind to one another

How can we be kind to one another in this classroom? In the school? In our neighborhoods and community?

How can we be unkind to one another in this classroom? In the school? In our neighborhoods and community?

Why is it important to be kind to one another?

What will we see if we are kind to one another? Hear? Notice?

How might kindness make you and your classmates better learners?

What are the best ways of working together?

Are you willing to take this challenge?

Rule 3: Be kind to this space

What is included in the words *this space?* (classroom, school, neighborhood, community)

How can we take care of and be kind to this space?

How can we be unkind to this space?

Why is it important to be kind to our space?

When we are kind to our space, what will we see? Hear? Notice?

How will kindness make this classroom a better place?

Are you willing to take this challenge?

Discussion

▷ Would you prefer to be a member of a classroom community that follows these three rules or one that does not? Why?

▷ If someone always followed these rules, would he or she be a successful person?

▷ How are these three rules good "life rules"?

Sample Three Basic Rules Chart

Kind to yourself

1. *I come prepared to learn.*
2. *I listen to others.*
3. *I ask for forgiveness.*

Kind to one another

1. *I play with everyone.*
2. *I give others compliments.*
3. *I have a lot of friends.*

Kind to this space

1. *I put my materials away.*
2. *I can find things easily.*
3. *The classroom stays clean.*

Not kind to yourself

1. *I can't find my materials.*
2. *I talk when others talk.*
3. *I carry a grudge.*

Not kind to one another

1. *I only play with certain friends.*
2. *I make fun of others.*
3. *I have a lot of fights.*

Not kind to this space

1. *There is a mess in my desk.*
2. *My stuff always gets lost.*
3. *We have to clean a long time.*

Learning the Kindness Pledge

Purpose   ▷ To ensure that students understand all the tenets of the
                      Kindness Pledge and can relate them to their everyday lives

Materials   ▷ Poster of the Kindness Pledge (see Appendix C)

                  ▷ Paper and pencil

                  ▷ Scissors

                  ▷ Two small containers

Preparation   ▷ If you wish, make a larger display of the Kindness Pledge.

                  ▷ Cut the paper into 18 slips (approximately 1 inch by 6 inches).
                      On 9 of the slips, write the numbers 1 through 9. On each of
                      the other 9, write one of the tenets of the Kindness Pledge.
                      Put each set of slips in a separate container.

Directions   1. Direct students' attention to the poster of the Kindness
                      Pledge, and ask for volunteers to read the 9 tenets aloud.

                  2. Ask students to suggest a real-life situation demonstrating
                      each of the tenets. If there are any tenets students don't
                      appear to understand, discuss to clarify.

                  3. After students have given a number of examples, tell them
                      that they have the opportunity to create a role play for each
                      of the tenets.

                  4. Have 9 of the students draw from the container with the
                      numbered slips. Have another 9 draw from the container with
                      the tenets. The students whose numbers and tenets match
                      become partners.

                  5. Explain that each pair will present a role play to illustrate the
                      tenets they have. Give the teams 15 to 20 minutes to design
                      and practice their role play.

                  6. Have the students form a semicircle, with a space for the role
                      plays at the front.

                  7. Ask each pair to perform. After each role play, ask the discus-
                      sion questions.

Discussion   ▷ Which tenet of the Kindness Pledge did the role players
                      demonstrate?

                  ▷ How could you tell?

                  ▷ Was the role play realistic?

                  ▷ What other situations come to mind that might demonstrate
                      this tenet?

▷ How can students and teachers live this tenet in their daily lives at school?

▷ Are you willing to live this challenge?

Building Integrity

Purpose   ▷ To introduce the concept of integrity: doing what you say you will do, doing your best, and following guidelines

Materials   ▷ Chalkboard or easel pad

Preparation ▷ None

Directions   1. Ask the students to suggest people in their lives they admire and wish they were like.

2. Ask the students to suggest the qualities and characteristics they admire in these people. (Possible responses include trustworthiness, honesty, caring, and so forth.) List these characteristics on the chalkboard or easel pad.

3. Ask students if they would still trust these people if they broke their promises, lied, or cheated.

4. Suggest that the word *integrity* means that you set standards for yourself and live according to a set of positive principles and values, even when there is no one there to remind you of what is right.

5. Suggest that people can be "out of integrity" with themselves. Ask the students for examples of how people might be out of integrity with themselves. Record these examples on the chalkboard or easel pad. For example:

   ▷ I make promises I don't keep.

   ▷ I don't do my chores on time.

   ▷ I don't clean my room without being asked.

6. Suggest that a person can be "out of integrity" with the other members of the class. Ask the students to suggest ways a person might be out of integrity with the class. Record these examples as well. For example:

   ▷ I don't follow the rules.

   ▷ I spread rumors and gossip.

   ▷ I don't participate in group activities.

7. Have students form groups of three. Ask the groups to create a brief story in which a person must make a difficult decision that reflects his or her integrity. Read the following as an example:

   > Sandy has begun to make friends with some students she thinks are really cool. Her parents won't be home until 7:00 P.M., and they expect her to have her homework done and start dinner before they get home. She

has one more day to complete a project. Her project partner is expecting Sandy to finish her part by tomorrow.

One of Sandy's new friends calls and invites her over to play video games. If Sandy doesn't go, the person might drop her. The person lives close by, and Sandy could get home before her parents do. Then Sandy's project partner calls. Sandy assures the partner that she'll get her part done.

8. When the groups are ready, ask one person from each group to read the group's story to the class. Ask the class to suggest what a person of integrity would do in the situation.

Discussion

▷ How would you define the word *integrity* to someone who doesn't know what it means? What examples could you give to illustrate?

▷ Is it possible to live up to your standards all the time? Why or why not?

▷ What happens when we don't live by our standards?

▷ If you get out of integrity with another classmate, how could you get back into integrity?

▷ If you get out of integrity with yourself, how could you get back into integrity?

A Code of Ethics

Purpose   ▷ To create a code of ethics based on people's mutual respect for one another

Materials   ▷ Chalkboard or easel pad

                  ▷ A large sheet of newsprint or poster board

                  ▷ Colored markers

Preparation   ▷ None

Directions   1. On the chalkboard or easel pad, write, in large letters, the following question for the group to consider: "What specifically would you see and hear if people respected one another?"

                  2. Facilitate class discussion of the question. Select a recorder to write down students' responses on the chalkboard or easel pad. Sample answers include the following:

                     ▷ We would listen to one another.

                     ▷ No one would be left out.

                     ▷ We would not put other people down.

                     ▷ We would help one another.

                     ▷ We would smile and say hello to everyone.

                  3. When the group runs out of answers, encourage them to examine the list they created.

                  4. Ask the group, "Which of these actions would be possible for you to do here at school?"

                  5. Circle (or in some other way identify) the actions the group would be willing to perform at school.

                  6. Ask for one or two volunteers to rewrite the identified responses neatly on the large sheet of newsprint or poster board.

                  7. Suggest that these statements are a "code of ethics," or a set of guidelines by which to live. Ask each class member to sign the code of ethics at the bottom.

                  8. Post the code of ethics in a prominent location in the classroom.

                  9. Ask the discussion questions 2 to 3 weeks after this activity.

Discussion   ▷ How do you feel we are doing in living up to our code of ethics?

                  ▷ Are we following the code of ethics as we intended it?

▷ What parts of this code are we following?

▷ Where do we need to make changes?

▷ What difference has following this code made in our classroom?

SEQUENCE 2

Who We Are

LESSONS

My Cultures

Purpose   ▷ To encourage students to examine their various personal cultures

Materials   ▷ A copy of each discussion round for each group of three students

Preparation   ▷ Photocopy Discussion Rounds 1–4.

Directions   1. Explain that everyone in the class belongs to many cultures: school, family, neighborhood, friendship, gender, and group (for example, basketball players, artists, tall students, short students).

2. Arrange students in groups of three.

3. Tell the groups they will have several "discussion rounds," in which they will talk about topics relating to different cultures. Hand out the copies of Round 1. Let students know that at the end of each discussion round, one person in each group will switch to another group, then they will have a new round.

4. Give the first groups time to discuss the questions in Round 1.

5. At the end of this round and each subsequent round, instruct one student in each group to move to a new group. (No group can re-create itself.)

6. Reassemble as a class and ask the discussion questions.

Discussion   ▷ What did you learn from examining your different cultures?

▷ On what basis do you find that a culture is unfairly treated?

▷ What would it take to stop the unfair treatment?

Discussion Round 1: Culture of School

1. What is your favorite memory from kindergarten through grade 3?
2. Are there any characteristics that would, in general, describe students who go to this school?
3. How is this school different from other schools in your area?
4. Who is a memorable teacher, coach, or other adult at this school?
5. Who is someone you would advise another student to look up to?
6. What are the symbols of this school?
7. Are there any celebrations or events that are special to this school?
8. What is a word, phrase, name, or statement about this school you never want to hear again?
9. Are there any examples of other schools' unfairly judging or treating this school or people from your school?
10. What might you need from people from other schools to stop treating you this way?

Discussion Round 2: Culture of Friends

1. In how many ways are the people in your circle of friends alike? Different?
2. What do you and your friends like to do together?
3. How might someone not in your group describe your group of friends?
4. Are there any special things you and your friends always do together? Clothes you wear? Places you go?
5. What will you want to remember about being with this group of friends years from now?
6. What is a word, phrase, name, or statement you never want to hear again about your group of friends?
7. Are there any examples of people not in your group unfairly judging or treating your group?
8. What might you need from people not in your group to stop treating your group this way?

Discussion Round 3: Culture of Males and Females

1. How are most males alike? Different?

2. How are most females alike? Different?

3. What traits and behaviors do you consider distinctively male? Distinctively female?

4. How do you think females might describe the culture of males?

5. How do you think males might describe the culture of females?

6. What is a word, phrase, name, or statement you never want to hear again about males? Females?

7. Are males unfairly treated? Are females unfairly treated?

8. What might you need from people of the opposite sex to stop treating your group this way?

Discussion Round 4: Family Cultures

1. What national or ethnic heritage do the members of your family share?

2. Does your family enjoy any special foods from your culture?

3. Does your family have any special ways of celebrating holidays?

4. What part of your physical appearance is a family trait?

5. What is a word, phrase, name, or statement you never want to hear again about your family?

6. What would you like others to know about your family?

7. Has your family ever been unfairly judged or treated?

8. What might you need from people to stop treating your family this way?

A Collage of My Culture

Purpose   ▷ To help students examine their personal and individual cultures, honor differences, and discover similarities

Materials   ▷ Chalkboard or easel pad
▷ Drawing paper
▷ Old magazines
▷ Scissors
▷ Glue
▷ Colored markers

Preparation   ▷ As a sample, create a collage depicting your own personal culture.

Directions   1. Distribute the drawing paper, magazines, and other supplies, and tell students you will be asking them to create a collage that illustrates their personal culture with respect to the following areas (write these on the chalkboard or easel pad):

▷ Race or ethnic heritage

▷ Religious background

▷ Language spoken at home

▷ Other languages spoken

▷ The language of your grandparents and great-grandparents

▷ The work your parents do and your grandparents or other ancestors did

▷ Special events and celebrations

▷ What you are proud of in your family

▷ What you'd like others to know about your family

2. Show the class the collage you made of your personal culture. Talk about all the aspects you chose to include. Let students ask questions.

3. Allow students time to work on their collages.

4. After students have finished their collages, ask them to form pairs. Ask each student to share his or her collage and talk about its meaning.

5. Have the students form groups of six to eight, and have them present their collages within their groups. Group members should listen without comment while the presenter describes

his or her collage, then ask questions about anything that intrigues them.

6. Reassemble the whole group for discussion.

Discussion

▷ What similarities did you notice you had with others? What differences?

▷ Did anything surprise you?

▷ Was there anything you thought of including in your collage but didn't?

▷ Did you find anything embarrassing?

▷ Did you worry if your partner or the group might laugh or not understand something you put in your collage?

Character Cards

Purpose   ▷ To demonstrate how easily we make judgments about others on the basis of appearances and what we have been told

Materials   ▷ Chalkboard or easel pad

                 ▷ Several 3-by-5-inch index cards (one card per student)

Preparation ▷ Create a deck of cards with one card for each student in your class. On one third of the deck write the word *loser,* on one third *neutral*, and on one third *winner.*

Directions   ### Part 1

1. Ask students if their classmates hold roles in the class: preppie, jock, nerd, geek, and so on.

2. List these roles on the chalkboard or easel pad, then ask the class to describe the characteristics of each role. List these as well.

3. From volunteers, select a group of students willing to portray these roles for the class. (As much as possible, let students select the roles they will play.)

4. Ask each student to present to the class how the character he or she chose looks, sounds, and acts. Presentations should be about a minute in length.

Part 2

1. Have the students form groups of five to eight students each.

2. Shuffle the deck of cards you have made. Tell students not to look at their cards, then give each student a card.

3. Suggest to the students that for the next few minutes they are to treat people in the following ways:

   ▷ If the card says *loser,* avoid them, pay no attention to them, and ignore their ideas.

   ▷ If the card says *neutral,* give them no special treatment.

   ▷ If the card says *winner,* treat them as though they are wonderful. Let them say and do whatever they want.

4. Ask the students to hold their cards up on their foreheads. In this way, everyone but the cardholder can see the card.

5. Ask the students to plan a fun activity for the class: a field trip, lunch out, or a movie. (Or pretend it is the first day of school and they are meeting their classmates after summer vacation.)

6. Let students discuss for about 10 minutes, treating one another as their cards suggest.

7. Stop the students. Have them put their cards facedown, making sure they don't look at them yet.

8. Ask students individually to describe how they were treated and felt, then to guess what type of card they held. After they do so, have them look at their cards.

Discussion

▷ How is this experience like everyday life in our class? In our school?

▷ How do you think people in our class and in our school choose whom to like? Is this fair?

▷ How should we choose the people we like and pay attention to?

▷ Is it necessary to like or agree with someone to include that person in your group or activity?

▷ What does this experience have to do with racism and discrimination of minority groups and other people with differences?

▷ How do you think racism and discrimination work?

▷ What is needed to end them?

Variation

With the deck of cards created in the activity, make smaller decks of 8 to 10 cards, then give the decks to different groups of students. Have the groups create skits demonstrating how students often treat one another negatively on the basis of roles. Challenge groups to create and enact solutions to the problems they create.

Power Circle

Purpose ▷ To encourage students to examine their values, beliefs, and actions, and to observe those of others

Materials ▷ None

Preparation ▷ Add any of your own ideas to the list provided in the lesson.

▷ Locate a large room with no furniture in which to hold the activity.

Directions *Part I*

1. Ask students to form a large circle, facing one another.

2. Ask one of the students to walk across the circle. Suggest to the group that this student has demonstrated one way of crossing the circle. Ask another student to cross in a different way. Ask every student to cross the circle using different movements—hopping, skipping, ways they invent.

3. When all have crossed, ask them to form groups of three with the people closest to them.

4. Ask each group to cross the circle together in a unique way, different from any other.

Part 2

1. When all the groups have crossed, ask students to cross the circle individually when they agree with or have had an experience you announce. Students should walk normally, without discussion or comments.

2. Selecting from the following list, give the following instructions, one at a time.

Cross the circle if you have ever . . .

enjoyed eating ice cream.

worried about flunking a test.

built a tree house.

lied to your parents.

cheated on a test.

taken the blame for someone else.

were made fun of because of how you look.

worried your parents might get a divorce.

lived with only one parent.

cleaned your room without being asked.

worried you would not be picked for a team.

spread rumors or gossip.

waited for a call that didn't come.

thought other people were more popular than you.

made fun of someone else.

worried about how you look.

thought your family was poor.

let someone convince you to do something you wish you hadn't.

apologized when you were wrong.

3. Next give these instructions.

Cross the circle if your family's ancestors came from . . .

Europe.

Asia.

North America.

South America.

Australia.

Africa.

South Sea Islands.

Caribbean Islands.

another part of the world.

Part 3

1. Ask one student to step forward. Ask every other student to this student's right to step forward. You have now formed two equal circles.

2. Ask the inner circle to turn and face the outer circle. Ask each person in the inner circle to move to the right until he or she is standing in front of a person in the outer circle.

3. Ask the pairs of students to interview each other by asking the following questions:
    ▷ What are five things you love about the music you listen to (favorite artists, recordings, songs)?
    ▷ What are three things you love to do when you have nothing to do?
    ▷ What are three ways you drive your family crazy?

4. Ask each person to introduce his or her partner to the group by giving the information gained.

Part 4

Note: No discussion questions are required for Part 4.

1. Re-form the large circle, with students facing the center.

2. Ask students to raise their right hands. Ask them to lower their right hands to the center of the chest of the person to their right.

3. Ask students to raise their left hands. Ask them to lower their left hands to the center of the chest of the person to their left.

4. Tell them to take the hands of the people they find beside them.

5. Suggest that the students belong to a class where everyone is honored, respected, and has equal rights. Suggest that, working as a community, they can accomplish many things. Point out that the quality of their school year depends on the quality of the relationships they build with one another.

Discussion   *Part 1*

▷ How did you feel crossing the circle by yourself? Was it hard to think of a new way to cross the circle?

▷ Did you ever feel silly?

▷ Was it harder or easier to walk across the circle in groups of three? Why or why not?

Part 2

▷ How did it feel to cross the circle with a lot of other people? With only a few other people?

▷ Were you surprised by who crossed the circle? Do you see any of your classmates differently now?

▷ Some of the suggestions were actions that break rules or challenge one's personal integrity. Is it okay to do these things because lots of others do? Why or why not?

▷ Some of the suggestions might have been embarrassing. Is it less embarrassing if you find out others do the same things? Why or why not?

Part 3

▷ Did you learn anything new about the people in our class?

▷ Did anything surprise you?

▷ Do people seem different now that you know more about them?

▷ What did it feel like to introduce someone to the group? To be introduced?

▷ Did you discover you had a lot of similarities? Differences?

Paper Beams

Purpose   ▷ To create a metaphor for diverse groups of people coming together to form a community

Materials   ▷ Five to 10 newspaper spreads per student

▷ A roll of masking tape for each group of 8 to 10 students

Preparation ▷ Make a sample cube and a sample pyramid by taping paper beams together.

▷ Locate a large room with no furniture in which to hold the activity.

Directions   1. Stand in front of the class. Roll up a stack of 5 to 10 newspaper spreads diagonally, from the bottom left corner to the top right corner. Tape this tube of tightly rolled paper in the middle.

2. Tell students this tube can be used as a beam to build a building. Suggest that they can use cubes or pyramids as the basic building blocks for a large structure.

3. Show the group your sample cube and pyramid to illustrate.

4. Divide the class into groups of 8 to 10.

5. Distribute the newspapers and tape.

6. Challenge each group to create a large structure, using all the paper they have. Each structure should be at least 7 feet tall.

7. Give students time to work. (Students may need more than one class period to complete their structures.)

8. When the structures are all finished, have the class form a circle around them. Suggest that the groups have created a village and that we are all part of one community.

Discussion   ▷ What did you learn from building your structures?

▷ Was it difficult working together?

▷ What did you learn about communication? Teamwork?

▷ When you stood back and looked at the whole room, were you surprised? What did you notice?

▷ What thoughts do you have now when you look at the newspaper village?

▷ How is this activity like life?

Variation The rolls of paper can also be bones, which can be used to create large skeletons of imaginary beasts. Challenge groups of students to create a menagerie of animal skeletons.

SEQUENCE 3

Circle of Kindness Meetings

LESSONS

Creating an Opening Ritual

Purpose
▷ To introduce the idea of the Circle of Kindness meeting and have small groups create a ritual that defines the beginning of each meeting

Materials
▷ Poster of the Circle of Kindness Meeting Agenda (see Appendix C)

Preparation
▷ If you wish, make a larger display of the Circle of Kindness Meeting Agenda.

▷ Enlist the aid of an adult leader for every group of 8 to 12 students.

Note: If possible, assign adult leaders to the same small groups during all Circle of Kindness meetings.

Directions
1. Explain to the class that, as part of the Kindness Initiative, students will participate in weekly Circle of Kindness meetings. These meetings are a time for small groups of students to express their feelings, clear up conflicts that arise among them, ask for forgiveness when needed, and look at different aspects of kindness and peacemaking within the classroom.

2. Show students the poster of the Circle of Kindness Meeting Agenda, and explain that, to begin, these meetings need a special ritual.

3. Ask students to give examples of any opening rituals they know about. For example:

   ▷ A team's putting their hands one on top of another in a circle before a game

   ▷ Members of a community service group reciting a pledge or singing a special song before a meeting

   ▷ Playing the national anthem before a baseball game

4. Divide the class into groups of 8 to 12 students, each with an adult leader. Let groups know they will be developing an opening ritual for their group. This could be a song, cheer, rap, or verse that in some way expresses the theme of kindness.

5. Challenge each group to create a ritual lasting no more than a minute to start each Circle of Kindness meeting. (Adult leaders provide help as needed.)

6. When the groups are finished, have them perform their rituals for the whole class.

Discussion

▷ What was it like for you to create an opening ritual for your group?

▷ Are the rituals you created fun? Meaningful?

▷ Are these rituals you will agree to use every time a Circle of Kindness meeting starts?

Checking In with Feelings

Purpose ▷ To give students the chance to tell their classmates how they are feeling and what level of trust they have with the group

Materials ▷ Poster of the Circle of Kindness Meeting Agenda (from Lesson 3.1)

▷ Slips of paper and pencils

Preparation ▷ Enlist the aid of your group leaders.

Directions 1. Have the class form their small groups, then with their group leader's assistance, perform their opening ritual.

2. Refer students to the poster of the Circle of Kindness Meeting Agenda, and explain that in this lesson they will learn how to "check in" with their feelings.

3. Direct students' attention to the second item on the agenda: checking in with feelings. Explain to the students that most feelings can be expressed by one of five words: *mad, sad, glad, scared,* and *guilty.* For example:

   ▷ I'm feeling *mad* because a friend of mine didn't send me an invitation to his party.

   ▷ I'm feeling *sad* because my grandmother is sick.

   ▷ I'm feeling *glad* because the sun finally came out.

   ▷ I'm feeling *scared* because I have a test this afternoon.

   ▷ I'm feeling *guilty* because I told my mom a lie.

4. Invite students, within their groups, to use one of these feeling words to tell the other group members how they are feeling and why, in one or two sentences.

5. After all the students have checked in with their feelings, explain that it is important for the members of each group to trust one another. Define *trust* as the sense of being safe in the group to share your feelings.

6. Ask the groups to discuss the level of trust they feel they have among their members. Students can indicate their level of trust by picking a number from one to seven, with one being very low and seven being extremely high.

Discussion ▷ Is it easy to talk about how we feel? If it is difficult, why?

▷ Why do you think it is important for each of you to express your feelings?

▷ Were you surprised at how someone else in your group felt?

▷ What level of trust do you think your group has?

▷ If low, what are the obstacles to greater trust? What can your group do to overcome them?

Clearing a Conflict, Asking for Forgiveness

Purpose   ▷ To teach students a four-point process that they can use to resolve a conflict and ask for forgiveness

Materials   ▷ Poster of the Circle of Kindness Meeting Agenda (from Lesson 3.1)

▷ Poster of the Four-Point Process for Clearing a Conflict and Asking for Forgiveness (see Appendix C)

Preparation   ▷ If you wish, make a larger display of the four-point process.

▷ Enlist the aid of your group leaders.

▷ Prepare two role plays between yourself and one of your group leaders—one to demonstrate how the four points are applied to clear a conflict and the other to show how they are used to ask for forgiveness. (For examples, see the role plays on page 153.)

Directions   1. Have students and their adult leaders get into their Circles of Kindness. Have them conduct their opening ritual and check in with their feelings.

2. Refer to the third step on the poster of the Circle of Kindness Agenda: clearing a conflict, asking for forgiveness. Suggest that anyone who is feeling angry or in conflict with another person or who needs to be forgiven by another person will have a hard time paying attention to what is going on in the classroom.

3. Refer students to the poster of the four-point process. Explain that students will learn how to use this process to help them clear up conflicts and ask for forgiveness.

4. With your adult partner, conduct your role plays of clearing a conflict and asking for forgiveness. Refer to the points on the poster as you do.

5. In the smaller groups, adult leaders ask students to look around and see if there is another student with whom they are in conflict or from whom they need to ask forgiveness. If no one volunteers, the leader may choose a student to help enact a role play of the group's choice. For example:

   ▷ You let your friend borrow your portable CD player. A teacher saw him listening to it and took it away for the rest of the semester.

   ▷ You and your friends at school laugh at a student you hang out with when you are at home in your neighborhood.

▷ You promised to take a book back to the library for your project partner, but you forgot, and the book is now over-due.

6. If the situation is about clearing a conflict, the leader asks the two students to stand up and face each other. The adult stands to the side to provide coaching if necessary.

7. The leader prompts the student who needs to clear a conflict as follows:

Point 1: State the *data. (What happened?)*

Point 2: State your *feeling. (Encourage students to use the words* mad, sad, glad, scared, *and* guilty.)

Point 3: State your *judgment. (Why do you think the situation happened?)*

Point 4: State your *choice. (What do you want from the other person?)*

8. For asking forgiveness, the leader brings the two students forward, then goes through the same process.

Discussion
▷ Why do you think it is important to talk about how you feel when you are in conflict with someone or need to ask forgiveness?

▷ Do you find you sometimes get angry with someone who does something to you that you have done to others? (For example, the person doesn't call you as promised, but you sometimes also forget to call when you promise.)

▷ What part of this four-part process is confusing? Scary? Uncomfortable?

▷ Where might you be able to use this technique outside of our Circles of Kindness?

Note
When doing the role plays, point out that conflicts may not always be resolved in a positive way and that people don't always accept apologies. The process is still worth trying, even though it might not have a positive outcome.

Sample Role Plays

Clearing a Conflict

Ray: John, will you listen to what I have to say?

John: Sure, Ray.

Ray: *(Data)* You promised to have lunch with me today. When I got to the cafeteria, I noticed you were sitting with some guys from your team. You didn't even save me a place.

(Feeling) I felt hurt, and then I got angry. I am still angry.

(Judgment) I thought you forgot about me and it wasn't important to you if we had lunch together or not.

(Choice) John, I want you to respect me and to do what you say you are going to do.

John: I'm sorry, Ray. I should have saved you a place. If you'd like, maybe we could have lunch together tomorrow. I'll wait for you, and we'll find a place together.

Ray: Thanks, John! See you then.

Asking for Forgiveness

Ray: *(Data)* The other day, I promised to have lunch with you. Some of my teammates asked me to sit with them, so I did. We got talking, and I forgot about us having lunch. When I saw you, I realized I had screwed up.

(Feeling) I felt really bad.

(Judgment) I should have left the group and come over to your table.

(Choice) I'd like it if we could have lunch together tomorrow.

John: Thanks for the apology, Ray. It would be great if we could have lunch tomorrow.

Creating a Closing Ritual

Purpose   ▷ To help students develop a closing ritual to indicate that the Circle of Kindness meeting has ended

Materials   ▷ Poster of the Circle of Kindness Meeting Agenda (from Lesson 3.1)

Preparation   ▷ Enlist the aid of your group leaders.

Directions   1. Have students and their adult leaders get into their Circles of Kindness and perform their opening ritual, check in with feelings, and use the four-point process to clear conflicts or ask for forgiveness, if necessary.

2. Refer students to the poster of the Circle of Kindness Meeting Agenda, and explain that in this meeting each group will create a closing ritual like the opening ritual they already have. For example:

   ▷ Each person says his or her name and extends a hand to the center. Each person places his or her hand on top of the others, as sports teams do in a huddle before a game.

   ▷ Students put their hands in the middle of the circle and take turns giving one another compliments. When everyone has received a compliment, students cheer, "Kindness! Kindness! Kindness!" and pull their hands back.

   ▷ Group members slap thighs, clap hands, and snap fingers, then all cheer, "Kindness rocks!"

3. Give the groups time to develop their closing rituals.

4. When the groups are satisfied with their closing ritual, have groups present their rituals to the class.

5. Let students know that they will use their closing rituals at the end of each future Circle of Kindness meeting.

Discussion   ▷ Why do you think our groups need a closing ritual?

   ▷ What does your ritual mean to your group?

   ▷ What did you like about other groups' rituals?

   ▷ Will you agree to use your rituals at the end of each Circle of Kindness meeting?

Kindness Pledge Activity

Purpose ▷ To strengthen the use of the Circle of Kindness meeting and enhance students' understanding of the first tenet of the Kindness Pledge: seeking the positive

Materials ▷ Poster of the Circle of Kindness Meeting Agenda (from Lesson 3.1)

▷ Poster of the Kindness Pledge (from Lesson 1.3)

▷ Materials listed for Lesson 4.1 (see page 159)

Preparation ▷ Enlist the aid of your group leaders.

▷ Make the preparations described for Lesson 4.1.

Directions 1. Have students and their adult leaders get into their Circles of Kindness and go through their routine: conduct their opening rituals, check in with feelings, and use the four-point process to clear conflicts or ask for forgiveness, if necessary.

2. Refer students to the poster of the Kindness Pledge, and let them know that in this lesson they will be learning about the first tenet of the pledge: seeking the positive.

3. Conduct Lesson 4.1.

4. Explain that from now on, the Circle of Kindness meetings will include an activity relating to the Kindness Pledge.

5. Ask the discussion questions, then have the groups perform their closing rituals.

Discussion ▷ What is it like to participate in Circle of Kindness meetings?

▷ Do you think talking about the tenets of the Kindness Pledge in these meetings is a good idea? Why or why not?

▷ What part of the meetings do you like best? Least?

▷ Is there anything you wish we could add to our meetings?

SEQUENCE 4

Living the Kindness Pledge

LESSONS

Seeking the Positive

Purpose
▷ To give students a chance to see what is positive about their classmates and to communicate that understanding through praise

Materials
▷ One large sheet of newsprint or easel-pad paper per student
▷ One set of colored markers and a roll of masking tape for every 8 to 10 students

Preparation
▷ Locate a large room without furniture in which to conduct the activity.

Directions
1. Give each person one sheet of newsprint or easel-pad paper and each group of 8 to 10 students one set of markers. Explain that the class will be making "praise capes."

2. Ask a student to help you demonstrate. Hold a sheet of paper on the student's back, then tape it to his or her back like a cape. With a marker, write a compliment on the student's cape.

3. Have students pair off to make similar capes.

4. Allow students to mingle and write positive comments on one another's capes. For example:
   ▷ You are friendly to everyone.
   ▷ You play a great game of volleyball.
   ▷ You are really good at math.

5. After 10 minutes, ask participants to go back to their original groups and return the markers to you.

6. Invite the students to show the class their capes.

7. Suggest to students that they hang their capes up on a class-room wall or bulletin board. Keep the capes up so students can write positive comments to one another for the rest of the week.

8. At the end of the week, let students take their capes home.

Discussion
▷ Who are the people in our lives we like to praise us?
▷ What about us do we want people to praise?
▷ Are there certain people who hurt us when they criticize us or put us down?
▷ What are some of the special ways people praise or compliment one another?

▷ What are the best compliments people put on your cape? Did any surprise you?

Variation   Ask pairs of students to trace each other's body shapes on large sheets of butcher paper. Post these "people banners" around the room. Let students write compliments to one another on the banners.

Putting Down Put-Downs

Purpose   ▷ To teach students a variety of ways of dealing with put-downs

Materials   ▷ Chalkboard or easel pad

Preparation   ▷ Arrange chairs in a semicircle, leaving an open space in which to conduct role plays.

Directions   1. Ask the class to describe all the ways students put each other down. List their responses on the chalkboard or easel pad. For example:

   ▷ Roll their eyes at their friends when you say something.

   ▷ Call you names.

   ▷ Walk away when you come up.

   ▷ Point at you and whisper to someone.

   ▷ Not let you join in a game.

2. Select two students to portray a situation in which one student puts the other down, using one of these examples. Suggest that the reaction of the student being put down should be hurt, anger, or both.

3. Give the two students a few minutes to plan, then have them perform the role play.

4. Ask for suggestions from the class as to how a person being put down in this type of situation could react in a positive way. List their responses. For example:

   Count from 1 to 10 before reacting.

   Breathe deeply.

   Say how you feel, using an "I" statement (for example, "When you call me that name, I feel angry and hurt, and I want you to stop doing that").

   Do not respond—just walk away.

5. Pair up the rest of the students. Ask each pair to prepare a short role play that demonstrates a different put-down situation.

6. Have students perform as many role plays as time allows. After each one, ask the following questions:

   ▷ Was the role play realistic?

   ▷ What techniques did the role player use to respond?

   ▷ Were these techniques effective?

   ▷ Could you use these techniques in your daily life?

Discussion

▷ Why do people put one another down?

▷ What is the effect of put-downs on our classroom community? On our school?

▷ What would happen if we didn't use put-downs?

▷ Will you commit to putting down put-downs?

Honoring Our Differences, Discovering Our Similarities

Purpose ▷ To allow students to honor the individual differences among their classmates and discover characteristics they have in common

Materials ▷ Chalkboard or easel pad

Preparation ▷ Locate a large room without furniture in which to conduct the activity.

Directions

1. Start with everyone in the middle of the room. Say to the group:

   I am going to ask you to sort yourselves into a series of smaller groups based on certain characteristics. Each time I name a characteristic, you must find all the people in the room that match you. For example, I might ask you to group yourselves by shoe size.

2. Have students who have the same shoe size form separate groups. Then say:

   Now that you are in groups with all the same shoe size, I'm going to ask you to find something out about the other members of your group. For example, I might ask you to find out what the person's favorite color is.

3. Have students find out about their favorite colors.

4. As time permits, have students form different groups based on the following characteristics (or ones you make up):

   All the people with the same eye color as you

   All the people with the same hair color as you

   All the people who like the same kind of pizza as you

   All the people born in the same month as you

5. After each group of students with similar characteristics forms, ask them to find out something different about the members of their group. For example:

   Favorite food or holiday

   The funniest, most unusual thing you can remember from grades K–3

   The most unusual thing you've ever seen while you were looking out a window of your home

   A teacher or coach you loved

Something you hope to accomplish someday

A place you'd like to visit

A dream you hold in your heart, even though it seems impossible

Discussion

▷ What similarities did you notice?

▷ What differences did you notice?

▷ Did you learn anything new about people you might have known for some time?

▷ Were you surprised about what you learned? In what way?

▷ How do you feel when you notice a lot of your classmates have similarities with you? When only a few do? When you are the only one who fits the description?

▷ Why are both similarities and differences important in a group of people?

Healing Our Hurts

Purpose   ▷ To challenge students to find ways to heal hurts among their classmates

Materials   ▷ Chalkboard or easel pad

▷ Poster of the Four-Point Process for Clearing a Conflict and Asking for Forgiveness (from Lesson 3.3)

Preparation   ▷ Arrange chairs in a semicircle, allowing an open space where students can conduct role plays.

Directions   1. Ask the students if they have ever hurt the feelings of others. Encourage them to describe specific situations. List these examples on the chalkboard or easel pad.

2. Direct students' attention to the poster of the four-point process:

   Point 1: State the *data. (What happened?)*

   Point 2: State your *feeling.*

   Point 3: State your *judgment. (Why do you think the situation happened?)*

   Point 4: State your *choice. (What do you want from the other person?)*

3. Let students know that they can use the four-point process to apologize at any time, not just when they are in their Circles of Kindness. Discuss steps they might want to use when they are not in the circle:

   Step 1: Decide if you have hurt someone.

   Step 2: Find a private time and space.

   Step 3: Use the four-point process to ask for forgiveness.

4. Have students form pairs. Ask each pair to create a role play showing one person apologizing to the other. For example:

   Data: I borrowed your library book, but I forgot to turn it in before the due date.

   Feeling: I'm really sorry. I feel guilty for doing that.

   Judgment: The book was in my locker under a bunch of papers.

   Choice: I plan on returning the book and paying the fine today.

5. Have pairs role-play as many situations as time permits. After each role play, ask the following questions:

    ▷ Was the role play realistic?

    ▷ Do you think the person would accept this apology? Why or why not?

Discussion

▷ How do you know when you have hurt someone's feelings?

▷ Would you forgive a person if he or she followed the four-point process?

▷ What are some ways someone has apologized to you? *(Responses may include giving you a gift, making you a card, giving you a note.)*

▷ What ways of apologizing did you like? Which ways might you use if you found you had hurt someone?

▷ Is there someone in your life you wish you could be friends with again? How could you rebuild the friendship?

Listening to One Another

Purpose	▷ To increase the ability of students to listen to other people
Materials	▷ Drawing paper and pencils
	▷ A hard surface for each student to use as a writing board (piece of heavy cardboard, binder, large book)
Preparation	▷ Locate a large room in which chairs can be moved into groups of three, facing outward.

Directions

1. Have the students form groups of three, and instruct them to sit back-to-back in a circle, facing outward. Give each student a sheet of drawing paper, a pencil, and a writing board.

2. Tell students you are going to call out a series of shapes for them to draw on the paper. They may put the shapes anywhere on their sheets—wherever they would like. Students should not look at one another's drawings. The shapes are as follows:

   ▷ A 2-by-2-inch cross

   ▷ A circle the diameter of a grapefruit

   ▷ A circle the size of a penny

   ▷ Two diagonal lines from one edge of the paper to the other

   ▷ Three squiggly lines going in the same direction

   ▷ A triangle 3 inches high

   ▷ A large square

   ▷ A small square

3. When students have finished, tell them that one of them will describe his or her drawing to the other two. These two will attempt to reproduce the drawing, sight unseen. This will mean that the first student's description will have to be very precise and the others will have to listen carefully. Students using the directions to reproduce the drawing may ask questions if they need to clarify.

4. Give each student two blank sheets of drawing paper. Have one student in each group describe his or her picture to the others while the other two draw. (You may wish to give a time limit.)

5. Repeat until each student's drawing has been reproduced.

6. When the drawings are finished, have students face one another and compare their drawings with the originals.

Discussion

▷ What happened while you were describing your drawing to the other students in your group?

▷ Did you find it easy or difficult to understand the descriptions as each student gave them?

▷ What did your drawings look like? How well were you able to reproduce the originals?

▷ What does this activity have to do with listening?

▷ Why is it important for people to listen carefully to one another?

Honoring Heroes

Purpose   ▷ To encourage students to identify and make closer connections with adults in their lives who will support them

Materials   ▷ Drawing paper
▷ Several colored markers for each student

Preparation   ▷ None

Directions   1. Give each student a sheet of drawing paper and several colored markers.

2. Instruct the students as follows:

> Draw a circle at the center of your paper, then write your name inside. Think of adults in your life whom you frequently see. These could be parents, teachers, coaches, or other people. Depending on how close you feel and how much you trust these various adults in your life, write their names close to your name or farther away. You can use different colored markers to write and decorate each name.

3. When students have finished their drawings, encourage them to share by asking the discussion questions.

Discussion   ▷ On your drawing, which people are close to you? Which ones are farther away?

▷ Why do you think some people are closer and some are farther away?

▷ Are there people you'd like to know better? How could you go about becoming closer to them?

▷ Whom would you seek out if you faced the following situations and needed to talk:

> You get a disappointing report card.
>
> You didn't make the team.
>
> A friend asks you to cheat on a test.
>
> A friend asks you to skip school.
>
> Someone of the opposite sex thinks you're cute and sends you a note.
>
> You have to choose which classes to take in the next grade.
>
> You feel overwhelmed and don't know what to do.

Variation   Encourage students to plan visits, make phone calls, and send letters, postcards, or e-mails to the people they want to thank and to those to whom they wish to be closer.

Reaching Higher for Success

Purpose   ▷ To help students learn the importance of setting goals and developing specific steps to achieve those goals

Materials   ▷ Scratch paper

▷ Success Action Plan (one copy per student)

▷ Chalkboard or easel pad

Preparation   ▷ Photocopy the Success Action Plan.

▷ Write the discussion questions on the chalkboard or easel pad.

Directions   1. Suggest that successful people have goals and make plans to achieve their goals. Ask students to suggest some doable goals they have in their lives. For example:

▷ Making a better grade in a certain class

▷ Saving for something you want to buy

▷ Getting on a team

2. Tell students that you want them to set a goal for themselves that can be achieved within 3 months.

3. Distribute the Success Action Plans.

4. Have students use scratch paper first to write down all the steps they will need to take and are willing to do to reach their goals.

5. Arrange the class in groups of three. Ask one person at a time to read his or her plans to the other two students. Ask the group to discuss the following questions after each person reads:

▷ Is the goal something you are likely to achieve?

▷ Are the steps specific enough to reach the goal?

▷ Are any steps left out?

▷ What evidence will you use to show you have achieved your goal?

6. After the discussion, have students list the final sequence of steps on their Success Action Plans.

7. Collect and review the Success Action Plans. Meet privately with any students who need to reset their goals or identify more specific steps, then return the plans to the students.

8. Review progress on the plans once a week during the Circle of Kindness meeting.

Discussion

▷ How many of you have fulfilled the goals you set? How many are still working on them?

▷ Do any of you want to create new goals?

▷ Did thinking through the specific steps you might need help you? If not, what do you need to reach the goal?

▷ Do you believe successful people set goals for themselves? Why might they do this?

▷ Do you know anyone—family member, friend, another adult—who sets goals and makes plans to achieve them?

▷ What happens when people have no goals or do not make good plans?

Success Action Plan

Name _____ **Date** _____

Goal you hope to achieve

_____

_____

_____

Three to five steps you are willing to take to complete this goal

_____

_____

_____

_____

_____

_____

_____

Evidence that will show you have achieved your goal

_____

_____

_____

_____

_____

_____

_____

_____

Cultivating Kindness in School: Activities That Promote Integrity, Respect, and Compassion in Elementary and Middle School Students.
© 2004 by Ric Stuecker. Champaign, IL: Research Press. (800) 519–2707.

Living Our Dreams

Purpose ▷ To encourage students to determine the kinds of contributions they plan to make to themselves, their families, and their communities

Materials ▷ Roles and Contributions worksheet (one copy per student)

Preparation ▷ Photocopy the Roles and Contributions worksheet.

Directions
1. Distribute the Roles and Contributions worksheets.
2. Ask students to examine the list of roles on the worksheet. Suggest that they play many roles now and will play more in the future. For each role that applies to them personally, ask them to write one specific contribution they can make.
3. Encourage students to share their worksheets with the class.

Discussion
▷ Do you believe it is possible for a single person or a small group of people to make major changes in the world?

▷ What people in your life are making a contribution? What are they doing?

▷ What people in the news are making a contribution? What are they doing?

Roles and Contributions

Name _____ **Date** _____

Role	Contribution
Family member	
Friend	
Team member	
Activity member	
Student	
Neighbor	
Worker	
Church or congregation member	

Cultivating Kindness in School: Activities That Promote Integrity, Respect, and Compassion in Elementary and Middle School Students.
© 2004 by Ric Stuecker. Champaign, IL: Research Press. (800) 519–2707.

SEQUENCE 5

Kindness Dilemmas

LESSONS

General Instructions
for Presenting Kindness Dilemmas

Purpose ▷ To create an opportunity for each student to make a moral decision about a perplexing situation and to compare his or her thinking with the thinking of other students

Materials ▷ The chosen Kindness Dilemma and related questions (one copy per student)

Preparation ▷ Photocopy the Kindness Dilemma.

Directions
1. Give each student a copy of the dilemma being discussed.
2. Ask students to read the dilemma silently and write the answers to the questions specifically relating to the story.
3. Go over the specific questions, one at a time, asking students for their responses to each.
4. When there are definite differences of opinions, create a debate with a spokesperson for each side of the argument.
5. Ask the general discussion questions, listed next.

Discussion
▷ Was the dilemma realistic?

▷ Have you ever had to make a decision in a similar situation? Could you share the situation and what you did?

▷ What is the kindest or most mature decision one could make in this situation?

▷ Is the kind or mature decision difficult? If so, why?

Jack's Dilemma

Jack and Ben hang out when they are in their neighborhood, but at school Jack hangs out with his friends on the basketball team. Jack likes Ben when he is home. He often goes over to Ben's house, and Ben comes over to his. Ben is not as good at sports as Jack is.

Jack is standing in the school hallway with his teammates. Ben comes out of the rest room. One of Jack's teammates makes a joke about Ben. All the boys laugh, then one of them says, "What a goof." And another says, "Yeah, what a geek."

Jack sees that Ben is looking at him. Someone from the team says, "Come on, Jack, let's get outta here."

Questions

1. What should Jack do?

2. Should Jack continue to be friends with the team?

3. Should Jack do anything when the team makes fun of his friend? Say anything to them later?

4. What should Jack say to Ben?

5. Should Ben continue to hang out with Jack?

Maria's Dilemma

Maria and Monica are good friends. They are in the cosmetics department of a large store. Maria notices Monica putting some very expensive cosmetics into her purse. Monica moves to another department and out the door while Maria continues to shop.

The store manager and security officer come up to Maria. The store manager says, "That's one of the kids who comes in here and shoplifts." They check Maria's purse but find no merchandise.

The security officer says, "Okay, you can go. But who is the girl you were with?"

Questions

1. Should Maria tell on Monica?

2. Is it ever okay to tell on a friend?

3. What if Maria's family are good friends with the store owner?

4. How bad is it to shoplift? How important is it not to shoplift?

5. What if Maria recently asked Monica to copy her homework—does that make a difference?

6. Is it okay to shoplift if you don't get caught?

Alicia's Dilemma

Alicia often stays after school to work with Ms. Wagner, her math teacher. Without this help, Alicia would probably fail the math class. Sometimes she helps Ms. Wagner clean up the classroom, and sometimes Ms. Wagner treats her to a soda.

Marjorie, Alicia's best friend, doesn't like Ms. Wagner at all. She thinks Ms. Wagner is mean and too tough on the class. One day in class, Marjorie slips a note to Alicia. In the note, she calls Ms. Wagner Ms. *Fag*ner and suggests that she is a lesbian.

Alicia chuckles when she reads the note, then hides it under her book. Looking up, Ms. Wagner says, "Alicia and Marjorie, are you two girls passing notes?"

Questions

1. Should Alicia lie and say she wasn't passing notes?

2. Should Alicia blame Marjorie since it was her note and Alicia was merely reading it?

3. What should Alicia say to Ms. Wagner?

4. How should Ms. Wagner handle this situation?

5. Should Alicia continue to stay for tutoring? Should Ms. Wagner continue to tutor Alicia?

6. What should Alicia say to Marjorie? Should they remain friends?

Cultivating Kindness in School: Activities That Promote Integrity, Respect, and Compassion in Elementary and Middle School Students.
© 2004 by Ric Stuecker. Champaign, IL: Research Press. (800) 519–2707.

Takisha's Dilemma

Takisha is helping Bonita make a list for Bonita's party. Takisha feels really special not only to be invited but also to help one of the most popular girls in the class. She feels accepted by the popular group. Takisha and Bonita are writing people's names down in the cafeteria during lunch. Another of Takisha's friends, Dorothy, sits down. Takisha says "Hi." Dorothy says, "What are you doing?"

Bonita frowns and folds up the list. She says, "Making a list for my birthday party, but *you're* not on it." Then she turns to Takisha and says, "Come over this afternoon and we'll finish up" and leaves the table.

Questions

1. What should Takisha say to Dorothy?

2. What should Takisha say to Bonita?

3. Should Takisha go to the party?

4. Should she remain friends with Bonita?

5. Is it okay to go to a party when some of your friends aren't invited?

6. What if not going to the party means Takisha will be left out of the popular group?

7. Is it okay to be friends with a group even if some of them are not nice to your other friends?

Cultivating Kindness in School: Activities That Promote Integrity, Respect, and Compassion in Elementary and Middle School Students.
© 2004 by Ric Stuecker. Champaign, IL: Research Press. (800) 519–2707.

Roberto's Dilemma

Sebastian is a great athlete. He is the key player on the basketball team. When Sebastian is not playing, the team has a hard time winning. The next game is the regional final against a really tough team, and the whole school is excited.

Sebastian might fail math. If he doesn't do well on the next test, the teacher might ask the coach to bench Sebastian. It is school policy that if a player's grade goes lower than a C during the semester, that person can't participate in extracurricular activities.

Roberto is smart, on the team, and a good friend of Sebastian's. Sebastian says to him the morning before the test, "I've studied all night, and I just can't get it."

Roberto says, "What do you want me to do?"

Sebastian says, "Just let me see your paper during the test so I can check my work. I'll only check to see if I've done it right."

The coach sees the boys in the hall and says, "I'm counting on you guys to pass that test—don't let me or the team down, guys."

Questions

1. What should Roberto do?

2. Is this really cheating?

3. What if Sebastian tells the other guys on the team that Roberto is going to make sure he passes the test? Should Roberto let him see his paper?

4. Should Roberto remain friends with a guy who asks him to do something dishonest?

5. Should the math teacher take Sebastian off the team if he fails the test?

6. How come cheating on the test is a big deal if no one gets hurt and Sebastian gets to play?

7. If they don't get caught, is it okay?

Creating Kindness Dilemmas

Purpose   ▷ To give students an opportunity to create stories that reflect the real-life dilemmas they face

Materials   ▷ Writing paper
                ▷ Chalkboard or easel pad
                ▷ Dilemma Sheet (one copy for every two or three students)

Preparation ▷ Write the criteria for the dilemma stories on the chalkboard or easel pad.
                ▷ Photocopy the Dilemma Sheet.

Directions 1. Suggest to the students that every day we must make decisions that affect ourselves and others.

2. Ask for suggestions of dilemmas students face in real life. For example:

   ▷ Someone puts down one of your friends.

   ▷ A friend asks you to do something you know is wrong.

   ▷ You have an opportunity to help someone.

3. Ask each pair or group of three students to create a story using the following criteria:

   ▷ Is one to three paragraphs long

   ▷ Focuses on one dilemma

   ▷ Is realistic

   ▷ Is simple

   ▷ Is perplexing

   ▷ Includes at least five questions that explore the dilemma

4. After giving students time to create their dilemma, ask each pair or trio to read their story and related questions to the group.

5. Ask if the group has any suggestions to make the story and questions better. In particular, ask whether the story meets the criteria.

6. Give each pair or trio a copy of the Dilemma Sheet. Have them make any changes and write out a final draft.

7. Collect the Dilemma Sheets.

8. Duplicate and use the students' dilemma stories as you choose, following the general instructions on page 179.

Discussion

▷ What was it like to make up your own dilemma?

▷ Were the stories you created typical of what you experience?

▷ Do you face many dilemmas in your life? When do they usually happen?

▷ When faced with a dilemma, how should you choose what to do? Would you talk it over with someone? If so, who?

▷ Has anyone ever asked your advice about a dilemma? If so, what happened?

▷ What makes some choices better or more mature than others?

Dilemma Sheet

Group members _____

_____

Our dilemma

_____

_____

_____

_____

_____

_____

Questions

1. _____

_____

2. _____

_____

3. _____

_____

4. _____

_____

5. _____

_____

APPENDIX A

The Context of Character Education

The Kindness Initiative is rooted in the research and theory of the character education movement. Over the past 30 years, compelling and research-based approaches to character education in youth have emerged. The first centers on developing *resiliency*. *Youth development* researchers have focused on fostering specific skills youth need to live healthy lives. *Asset building,* the approach favored by the Search Institute of Minneapolis, has identified 40 basic developmental necessities in eight areas that youth need during their first two decades of life. Support for *student aspirations* is another approach toward character education in youth.

Resiliency

Resiliency researchers look for traits and characteristics of children who come from situations of adversity and tragedy, yet who adapt successfully. Schools and classrooms that tend to produce resilient youth are often characterized by caring relationships, high expectations, and opportunities to participate (Benard, 1997). The concept of resiliency has been applied to all children. Its development is predicated on the quality of relationships between children and influential adults in their lives.

Resiliency refers to an ability to spring back, rebound, and/or successfully adapt in the face of adversity stemming from the environment, personal trauma and tragedy, or emotional disability (Henderson, 1997). Every young person (indeed, every person of any age) needs to develop resiliency.

Resilient youth exhibit high self-esteem and have a belief in their own efficacy, a repertoire of solution-finding skills, and the ability to critically analyze situations and think creatively. They tend to be achievement oriented, socially connected, future focused, and sensitive to personal boundaries. They seek help when needed and withdraw from negative situations.

According to Henderson and Milstein (1996), research suggests that to promote resiliency schools should take the following actions.

Provide opportunities for meaningful participation

▷ Students are viewed as workers, and teachers are viewed as coaches.

▷ Everybody's contributions are seen as important.

▷ Members grow and learn by sharing and treating one another with respect.

▷ Potentially positive new experiences are encouraged.

Increase prosocial bonding

▷ A positive and supportive organizational climate and culture exist.

▷ Equity and reasonable risk taking and learning are promoted.

▷ Visions and missions are clearly communicated and agreed upon.

Set clear, consistent boundaries

▷ Cooperation and support exist.

▷ Schoolwide objectives are shared.

▷ Members are involved in setting policies and rules.

Teach life skills

▷ Efforts are made to improve the school.

▷ Sensible risk taking is supported, as are individual and group skill development.

▷ Positive role modeling is practiced.

Provide caring and support

▷ Members have a sense of belonging.

▷ Cooperation is promoted.

▷ Celebrations of success are practiced.

▷ Leaders spend lots of positive time with members.

▷ Resources are obtained with a minimum of effort.

Set and communicate high expectations

▷ Individual efforts are viewed as important.

▷ Reasonable risk taking is promoted.

▷ A "can do" attitude prevails.

▷ Individualized growth plans are developed and monitored.

With its emphasis on caring and empowering relationships, the resiliency approach seeks to support vulnerable youth with both one-to-one and group activities.

Youth Development

Youth development focuses on the needs and competencies of growing young people. Dr. Peter L. Benson of the Search Institute writes:

> Youth development is an emerging and somewhat eclectic conceptual framework seeking to define the skills and competencies youth need to be successful in a rapidly changing world. It is more a philosophy than an area of direct, integrated scientific inquiry. Youth development practitioners advocate paying attention to needs, skills and competencies during the second decade of life, with an accent on organizing youth programs, schools and community policy to be particularly responsive to engagement, belonging, connection and empowerment. (Benson, 1997, p. 21)

The youth development approach has as its strength and focus the fostering of specific competencies and skills through activities, programs, and curricula.

Developmental Assets

Benson (1997) and his colleagues at the Search Institute have identified 40 external and internal developmental assets, or positive experiences and qualities, that have tremendous influence on young people's lives. This philosophy includes anyone touching the lives of youth. Families, schools, neighborhoods, congregations, institutions, and individuals in a community can play a role in building assets in youth.

The assets are divided into eight areas (Roehlkepartain, 1999). Specifically, the guidelines for asset building in youth are as follows:

1. SUPPORT them with your love, care, and attention.(Assets 1–6)
2. EMPOWER them with opportunities to make a difference in their family and community. (Assets 7–10)
3. Establish clear BOUNDARIES and have high EXPECTATIONS. (Assets 11–16)
4. Help them engage in activities that make CONSTRUCTIVE USE OF TIME. (Assets 17–20)
5. Nurture in them a COMMITMENT TO LEARNING. (Assets 21–25)
6. Instill POSITIVE VALUES to guide them. (Assets 26–31)
7. Help them develop life skills and SOCIAL COMPETENCIES. (Assets 32–36)
8. Nurture, celebrate, and affirm their POSITIVE IDENTITY. (Assets 37–40)

In *The Troubled Journey,* Benson (1993) listed the following challenges for educators:

- ▷ Personalize schools so that each and every child feels cared for, supported, and important.
- ▷ Enhance social competencies, including friendship-making skills, caring skills, assertiveness skills, and resistance skills.
- ▷ Emphasize the development of positive values, particularly those that build a sense of personal responsibility for the welfare of others.
- ▷ Offer quality prevention programming in multiple areas of risk, including alcohol, tobacco, illicit drugs, depression and suicide, sexuality, and vehicle safety.
- ▷ Enhance academic effectiveness to ensure that students at all income levels gain in academic motivation and competence.
- ▷ Emphasize service learning programs and seek to provide all students with helping opportunities and personal reflections on the meaning of helping.
- ▷ Provide strong support services for youth at risk.

The research of the Search Institute suggests that when youth have few of these assets in their lives, their vulnerability to alcohol abuse, sexual activity, and violent and antisocial behaviors goes up. This vulnerability dramatically decreases as the number of assets increases. According to the research of the Search Institute, the average sixth through twelfth grader surveyed possesses only 18 of the 40 assets. Only 8 percent of young people have 31 to 40 assets (Roehlkepartain, 1999).

The strength of the asset-building approach is in its delineation of 40 developmental assets and its community-based approach. This approach seeks to unite home, school, and community in creating a culture that values the young on their journey to adulthood.

Student Aspirations

Although the asset-building approach has been extremely popular as a general direction and philosophy, it has proven difficult to create specific programming that incorporates asset building in the classroom. Russell J. Quaglia and Kristine M. Fox describe a more teacher-friendly and classroom specific approach. This approach identifies eight asset-building conditions that teachers can promote to raise student aspirations, defined as an individual's ability to identify and set goals for the future while being inspired in the present to work toward those goals.

In their research, Quaglia and Fox (1998) found that many students had a discordance between their inspiration and their motivation toward working to achieve those goals. Over and over, students described their aspirations this way:

I want to be a doctor, but I don't like science.

I want to be a community leader, but I don't like too much responsibility.

I want to go to college, but I don't like to study.

As described in *Student Aspirations: Eight Conditions That Make a Difference* (Quaglia & Fox, 2003d), the eight conditions lead students not only to construct hopes and dreams but also to acquire the motivation and discipline to achieve their goals.

The eight conditions are arranged hierarchically in three clusters:

Building a foundation for raising student aspirations: Belonging, heroes, sense of accomplishment

Motivating students and instilling enthusiasm in the classroom: Fun and excitement, curiosity and creativity, spirit of adventure

Establishing the mind-set students need in order to aspire: Leadership and responsibility, confidence to take action

Books for three different grade levels (K–5, 6–8, and 9–12) include classroom activities that give teachers the opportunity to integrate this common sense approach directly into the curriculum (Quaglia & Fox, 2003a, 2003b, 2003c).

References

Benard, B. (1997). Resiliency research: A foundation for youth development. *Resiliency in Action, Winter,* 13–18.

Benson, P. L. (1993). *The troubled journey.* Minneapolis: Search Institute.

Benson, P. L. (1997). Connecting resiliency, youth development, and asset development in a positive-focused framework for youth. *Resiliency in Action, Winter,* 19–22.

Henderson, N. (1997). Resiliency and asset development: A continuum for youth success. *Resiliency in Action, Winter,* 23–27.

Henderson, N., & Milstein, M. (1996). *Resiliency in school: Making it happen for students and educators.* Thousand Oaks, CA: Corwin Press.

Quaglia, R. J., & Fox, K. M. (1998). *Believing in achieving.* Orono, ME: National Center for Student Aspirations.

Quaglia, R. J., & Fox, K. M. (2003a). *Raising student aspirations: Classroom activities for grades K–5.* Champaign, IL: Research Press.

Quaglia, R. J., & Fox, K. M. (2003b). *Raising student aspirations: Classroom activities for grades 6–8.* Champaign, IL: Research Press.

Quaglia, R. J., & Fox, K. M. (2003c). *Raising student aspirations: Classroom activities for grades 9–12.* Champaign, IL: Research Press.

Quaglia, R. J., & Fox, K. M. (2003d). *Student aspirations: Eight conditions that make a difference.* Champaign, IL: Research Press.

Roehlkepartain, E. C. (1999). *You can make a difference for kids.* Minneapolis: 3M Corporation and Search Institute.

APPENDIX B

The High School Connection

It is very helpful to connect the elementary and middle school Kindness Initiative with a team of high school students who can work both on the task force and in classrooms. The high school students serve as role models for the younger students, aid teachers during activities, and run some activities on their own. The following brief discussion outlines the high school connection and includes suggestions for programming: a bonding retreat, leadership classes, and other special training.

One or two adults sponsor and guide the high school team. One of these adults needs to be a staff member at the high school; the other could be a community volunteer. These adults are responsible for choosing the high school team, attending the bonding retreat, overseeing the training, and holding debriefing sessions with high school team members after each Kindness Initiative experience. Students are required to maintain their usual grade-point average; attend all meetings, activities, training sessions, and debriefings; and use appropriate language and manners with one another and with younger students.

Basic guidelines for selection are as follows:

▷ Make students from all grade levels eligible.

▷ Balance the number of boys and girls.

▷ Avoid selecting only those who are seen as natural leaders. Rather, select and recruit students from many constituencies among the student population.

▷ Select a team of 20 to 25 students.

Bonding Retreat

It is important for the high school students to become a team that sees itself as a distinct, positive, and supportive group. A bonding retreat is helpful in realizing these goals. Adults can create their own retreat or hire an outside trainer to create a bonding experience. Either way, the retreat should include the following components:

Ice-breakers: Low-risk activities in which students learn one another's names, intermingle, and play

Team-building challenges: Activities that challenge the team to work together to find solutions

Self-disclosure activities: Small-group activities in which students open up about who they are inside and connect with one another on a more personal basis

Commitments: An exploration of program requirements, the scope of the program, and program responsibilities, as well as a opportunity to ask students to sign commitment statements

Leadership Programs and Other Special Training

In addition to the bonding retreat, leadership classes and other special training are essential to keep students' motivation high and their skills current. Many excellent leadership programs are available, and the high school team's participation in a one-semester leadership course is desirable.

Some schools create a large pool of leaders from which they can then draw, and others create an oversight board of veteran leaders and adult sponsors to guide the leadership teams.

Schools generally find it helpful to meet monthly for the following purposes:

▷ To reconnect students to the leadership program

▷ To create new bonds with veterans and new leaders

▷ To overview and inservice new programs and activities

▷ To debrief recent experiences

▷ To plan new leadership initiatives

The leadership class can foster programs such as peer mediation, peer tutoring, peer assistance, project graduation, project prom, and other asset-building programs the team and its sponsors select. The curriculum can be based on the following resources. Other opportunities for youth development and training are also often available locally.

Building Assets Together: 135 Group Activities for Helping Youth Succeed, by Jolene L. Roehlkepartain. Minneapolis: Search Institute (1997).

Creating the Peaceable School: A Comprehensive Program for Teaching Conflict Resolution (2nd ed.), by Richard J. Bodine, Donna K. Crawford, and Fred Schrumpf. Champaign, IL: Research Press (2002).

How to Create Positive Relationships with Students: A Handbook of Group Activities and Teaching Strategies, by Michelle Karns. Champaign, IL: Research Press (1994).

Girls' Circle Facilitator Training: Promoting Resiliency and Self-Esteem in Adolescent Girls, by Giovanna Raormina and Beth Hossfeld. Mill Valley, CA: Girls' Circle (1999).

The Incredible Indoor Games Book, by B. Gregson. Belmont, CA: Pitman Learning (1982).

Peer Mediation: Conflict Resolution in Schools (Rev. ed.), by Fred Schrumpf, Donna K. Crawford, and Richard J. Bodine. Champaign, IL: Research Press (1997).

Reach for the Stars: A Mentoring Project for High School and Grade School Girls, by Rosemary Richards. Louisville, KY: Unpublished manuscript (1999). (Available from the author at Sacred Heart Academy, 3175 Lexington Rd., Louisville, KY 40206.)

Reviving the Wonder: 76 Activities That Touch the Inner Spirit of Youth, by Ric Stuecker with Suze Rutherford. Champaign, IL: Research Press (2001).

APPENDIX C

Kind Classrooms Lesson Posters

Three Basic Rules

Rule 1: Be kind to yourself.

Rule 2: Be kind to one another.

Rule 3: Be kind to this space.

Cultivating Kindness in School: Activities That Promote Integrity, Respect, and Compassion in Elementary and Middle School Students.
© 2004 by Ric Stuecker. Champaign, IL: Research Press. (800) 519–2707.

Kindness Pledge

We are kind to one another by . . .

1. Seeking the positive

2. Putting down put-downs

3. Honoring our differences

4. Discovering our similarities

5. Healing our hurts

6. Listening to one another

7. Honoring heroes

8. Reaching higher for success

9. Living our dreams

Cultivating Kindness in School: Activities That Promote Integrity, Respect, and Compassion in Elementary and Middle School Students.
© 2004 by Ric Stuecker. Champaign, IL: Research Press. (800) 519–2707.

Circle of Kindness Meeting Agenda

1. Opening ritual

2. Checking in with feelings

3. Clearing a conflict, asking for forgiveness

4. Kindness Pledge activity

5. Closing ritual

Cultivating Kindness in School: Activities That Promote Integrity, Respect, and Compassion in Elementary and Middle School Students.
© 2004 by Ric Stuecker. Champaign, IL: Research Press. (800) 519–2707.

Four-Point Process for Clearing a Conflict and Asking for Forgiveness

Point 1: State the data.

Point 2: State your feeling.

Point 3: State your judgment.

Point 4: State your choice.

Resources

Angell, M. C. (1966). *My spirit flies: Portraits of women in their power.* Bellingham, WA: Bay City Press.

Armstrong, T. (1994). *Multiple intelligences in the classroom.* Alexandria, VA: Association for Supervision and Curriculum Development.

Armstrong, T. (1998). *Awakening genius in the classroom.* Alexandria, VA: Association for Supervision and Curriculum Development.

Benson, P. L. (1997). *All kids are our kids: What communities must do to raise caring and responsible children and adolescents.* San Francisco: Jossey-Bass.

Benson, P. L. (1998). *What kids need to succeed: Proven, practical ways to raise good kids.* Minneapolis: Free Spirit.

Bodine, R. J., Crawford, D. K., & Schrumpf, F. (2002). *Creating the peaceable school: A comprehensive program for teaching conflict resolution* (2nd ed.). Champaign, IL: Research Press.

Brown, J. L., & Moffett, C. (1999). *The hero's journey: How educators can transform schools and improve learning.* Alexandria, VA: Association for Supervision and Curriculum Development.

Crockett, L., & Smink, J. (1991). *The mentoring guidebook: A practical manual for designing and managing a mentoring program.* Clemson, SC: National Dropout Prevention Center.

Emery, M., & Purser, R. E. (1996). *The search conference: A powerful method for planning organizational change and community action.* San Francisco: Jossey-Bass.

Goldstein, A. P., Glick, B., & Gibbs, J. C. (1998). *Aggression Replacement Training: A comprehensive intervention for aggressive youth* (Rev. ed.). Champaign, IL: Research Press.

Gregson, B. (1982). *The incredible indoor games book.* Belmont, CA: Pitman Learning.

Karns, M. (1994). *How to create positive relationships with students: A handbook of group activities and teaching strategies.* Champaign, IL: Research Press.

Karns, M. (1995). *DOisms: Ten prosocial principles that ensure caring connections with kids.* Sebastopol, CA: National Training Associates.

Karns, M. (1998). *Ethnic barriers and biases: How to become an agent for change.* Sebastopol, CA: National Training Associates.

Kornfield, J., & Kornfield, C. F. (1996). *Soul food: Stories to nourish the spirit and the heart.* New York: HarperCollins.

Lewis, B. A. (1997). *The kid's guide to service projects: Over 500 projects for young people who want to make a difference.* Minneapolis: Free Spirit.

Lewis, B. A. (1998). *The kid's guide to social action: How to solve the social problems you choose—and turn creative thinking into positive action.* Minneapolis: Free Spirit.

Lewis, B. A. (1998). *What do you stand for? A kid's guide to building character.* Minneapolis: Free Spirit.

McGinnis, E., & Goldstein, A. P. (1997). *Skillstreaming the elementary school child: New strategies and perspectives for teaching prosocial skills* (Rev. ed.). Champaign, IL: Research Press.

Pipher, M. (1994). *Reviving Ophelia: Saving the selves of adolescent girls.* New York: Ballantine.

Quaglia, R. J., & Fox, K. M. (2003). *Raising student aspirations: Classroom activities for grades K–5.* Champaign, IL: Research Press.

Quaglia, R. J., & Fox, K. M. (2003). *Raising student aspirations: Classroom activities for grades 6–8.* Champaign, IL: Research Press.

Quaglia, R. J., & Fox, K. M. (2003). *Raising student aspirations: Classroom activities for grades 9–12.* Champaign, IL: Research Press.

Quaglia, R. J., & Fox, K. M. (2003). *Student aspirations: Eight conditions that make a difference.* Champaign, IL: Research Press.

Roehlkepartain, E. C. (1999). *You can make a difference for kids.* Minneapolis: 3M Corporation and Search Institute.

Roehlkepartain, J. L. (1997). *Building assets together: 135 group activities for helping youth succeed.* Minneapolis: Search Institute.

Rolzinski, C. A. (1990). *The adventure of adolescence: Middle school students and community service.* Washington, DC: Youth Service Alliance.

Stuecker, R., with Rutherford, S. (2001). *Reviving the wonder: 76 activities that touch the inner spirit of youth.* Champaign, IL: Research Press.

Weisbord, M. R., & Janoff, S. (1995). *Future search: An action guide to finding common ground in organizations and communities.* San Francisco: Berrett-Koehler.

About the Author

Ric Stuecker, M.A., has taught school at every level—elementary through college. For the past 15 years he has been a nationally recognized educational trainer, consultant, and speaker. He has dedicated his life to challenging youth to discover their inner strength and spirit and to make significant contributions to the community and world outside themselves. Since he was a young teacher, he has believed it is crucial for adults to mentor youth and initiate them in meaningful ways into the adult community.

With Suze Rutherford, Ric is author of the book *Reviving the Wonder: 76 Activities That Touch the Inner Spirit of Youth* (Research Press, 2001). He has also led workshops in leadership, personal growth, study skills, and communication skills throughout the United States. He has trained adults who teach and work with youth in resiliency and asset building, nonverbal communication and management, and presentation skills. He has directed a treatment center for drug dependent youth and has been a consultant to a number of schools and school districts holding grants from the Office of Safe and Drug-Free Schools.

Last year, Ric returned to the classroom to teach seventh and eighth grade students at Our Lady of Mount Carmel School in Louisville, Kentucky. He lives in Louisville with his wife, Barbara, and has two grown daughters.